Scrapbooking Techniques

Contents

Introducing scrapbooking

Modern scrapbooking is a rapidly growing craft geared at teaching the preservation of photographs and capturing life's significant moments through words or 'journalling'. The art of scrapbooking combines the principles of photograph preservation with the principles behind the design of an appealing layout.

HISTORY

Scrapbooking began several hundred years ago, when people used diaries, journals and hand-made albums to record thoughts, recipes, poetry and quotes. The earliest surviving book dates from the seventeenth century in Germany.

Throughout history, artists and other creative thinkers have kept scrapbooks of drawings, ideas and text. Among them was the great Renaissance artist and scientist, Leonardo da Vinci. Amazingly,

many of his pages have been the inspiration for today's printed papers, vellum and rubber stamps.

References to 'common-place books' appear as early as the 1590s. These included collections of diary entries, drawings and newspaper clippings.

Even Shakespeare's play Hamlet mentions the recording of notes in a commonplace book. In 1706, the British philosopher John Locke published his New Method of Making Commonplace Books, which advises readers on the best way to preserve ideas, proverbs, speeches and other notes. By 1825, the term 'scrapboook' was in use and a magazine devoted to the hobby, The Scrapbook, was in circulation.

In the late nineteenth century, scrapbooks attained popular status and many magazines published ideas on what to include in them. Mementos, such as newspaper clippings, pressed flowers, calling cards, letters, ribbons and locks of hair, all found their way into personal scrapbooks. Pictures were etched or engraved onto the pages.

During the Victorian era, even more embellishments were added to scrapbook pages, such as ornamental vignettes and cut-outs. Die-cuts (pre-cut paper shapes) and stamps were introduced in the 1870s and companies manufactured images specifically for inclusion in these albums.

In the late nineteenth century, the invention of the camera added a new dimension to the art of scrapbooking. As photography became more widespread and affordable, photographs began to appear in scrapbook albums.

During the 1880s, an increased focus on the study of genealogy–the identification and preservation of family roots–gave scrapbooking another new direction. This fascination continues today as many families research their genealogies as a means of discovering connections to the past and preserving the family heritage for the future.

Today's scrapbooks may vary greatly from those of the 1500s. The manner in which they are presented and preserved has evolved, reflecting the knowledge of preservation and archival techniques. However, one common thread connects the past to the present–scrapbooks have always told a story.

SCRAPBOOK OCCASIONS

Many scrapbookers begin with a particular event in mind: a baby is born, or someone in the family is getting married, starting school, having a significant birthday, graduating, retiring or experiencing hard times, such as the death of a loved one. Once a goal or reason has been established, it is time to sort through photographs and memorabilia, organizing them and then ordering them to tell a story.

The great thing about scrapbooking is that anyone can do it. The only prerequisites are being able to cut and paste. This craft appeals to all age groups. Children love to get involved and kids can scrapbook.

The creation of a scrapbook can bring families together as they share highlights and rekindle memories. Children enjoy looking through family scrapbooks, especially when events meaningful to them are scrapbooked and journalled.

Scrapbooking the difficult or sad times, like divorce, death, moving, or any major change in the family structure, can even help children and adults. The pages of the scrapbook, with patterns made from colours, shapes and textures, emphasize that life is an imperfect but dynamic mixture of events and emotions.

A scrapbook can be created for any theme: a year album, baby album, heritage album or school album. Albums can also display an individual's collections, such as cars, teacups, teddy bears, quilts, letters or postcards.

Many businesses, from florists to restaurants, use scrapbooks to showcase their various products and services.

Albums can be created as special gifts, such as mini brag (baby) books, kitchen tea (recipe) collections, wedding anniversary and birthday books.

The beauty of this craft is that there is no right or wrong. Scrapbooking should be a meaningful experience for the creator, free from judgment or critique.

The selection of photographs, papers, embellishments and journalling should reflect the scrapbooker's own personality and their taste.

Modern scrapbooking is a communal pastime. Scrapbooking shops often support groups of scrapbookers by providing access to shop equipment. Scrapbookers derive the practical benefit of sharing costly equipment, such as punches and tools, as well as finding inspiration and mutual interests. It's also a great way to make new friends.

The ideas and techniques shared in this book will provide the beginner or experienced scrapbooker with the inspiration and knowledge to create a wonderful album, filled with mementos for the family and future generations.

Materials and equipment

When you are first assembling your scrapbooking materials you will start with the most basic cutting and pasting tools, but the scope of the craft is so wide that a fantastic range of materials and equipment can be utilized in the creation of each page. Specialist products are available from scrapbooking stores.

PAPER

All paper used for scrapbooking should be acid and lignin free. Cardstock is a thick, sturdy paper that can be used to hold all the elements of a page together. Printed paper tends to be thinner. Photographs are either directly mounted (attached) onto cardstock or matted (adhered to layers of paper) first, then mounted. Cardstock is available in more than 400 colours and numerous textures. Printed papers also come in a wide variety, including hearts, animal prints, floral, lace, water, checks and stripes.

As current scrapbooking trends have originated in the USA all sizes for scrapbooking are in inches. The most common paper size is 12 x 12 inches or 30.5 x 30.5 cm. Other sizes are available, such as 8 $^{1}/_{2}$ x 11 inches or 21.5 x 27 cm, but selections in patterned papers are somewhat limited.

ADHESIVES

Any adhesive used in a scrapbook must be acid free. Some adhesives allow for items to be shifted, others set quickly.

Options include glue dots, bottled glue, glue sticks, liquid glue pens and silicone glue. Photo tape has a peel-off backing and double-sided tape comes on a tape roller. Adhesive photo corners are useful.

A good choice for a novice scrapbooker is the double-sided tabs that come in a box or dispenser. The advantage is that they are refillable and cost effective.

Glue sticks are great for children, due to ease of use and reasonable pricing.

The choice of adhesives also depends on what is being attached, its size and weight. Fabric is best attached with an acid-free craft glue (PVA). Silicone glue is great for tiny items but heavy items such as pockets or foam core require strong glues.

PENS

A pen or marker used in a scrapbook must be of archival quality, waterproof, fade resistant, non-bleeding and acid free.

Pens used in scrapbooking are made from pigment ink; therefore the ink is permanent. When starting, a good-quality black pen with a monoline nib is essential for journalling.

There are several varieties of pens available. These include monoline, calligraphy or chisel point, brush, scroll, and gel pens. There is also a red-eye pen that is used for removing the red from peoples' eyes in photos.

The Vanishing Ink Pen is filled with special ink that will vanish off the pages within 24-72 hours. It is a great alternative to the lead pencil as it will not leave any stray marks. The full range of pens will be discussed in the Using Pens section of this book.

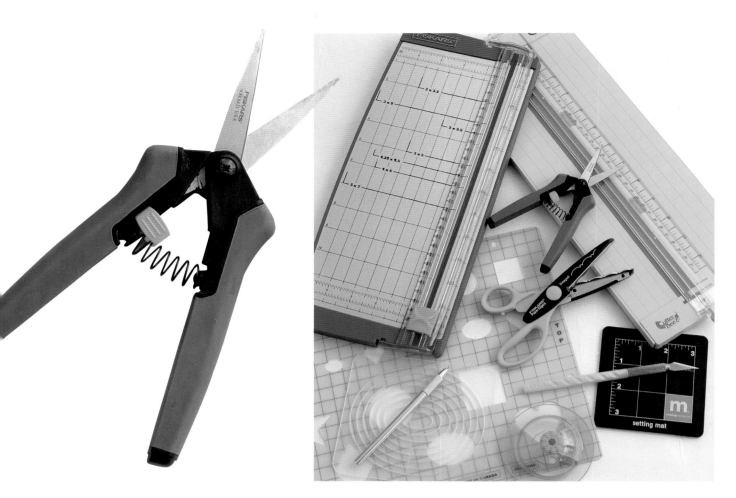

CUTTING TOOLS

Scissors are used extensively in scrapbooking so purchasing a sturdy, sharp pair of paper scissors will prove to be a valuable investment.

Every scrapbooker should also invest in a paper trimmer. A 30.5 cm (12-inch) paper trimmer is recommended as it will provide a sufficient cutting surface for an entire sheet of the standard 30.5 cm (12-inch) square cardstock. There are many different brands on the market today. The most versatile paper trimmers have an extension ruler and a few different types of blades for scoring and for perforating.

Fancy scissors are often used to create different edges. They can be purchased in a wide variety of styles.

Cutting systems have also been developed to help in cutting shapes like circles and ovals. Many of them can cut a variety of shapes as well as letters of the alphabet.

PAGE PROTECTORS

It is important to place completed pages directly into a page protector to prevent people touching and damaging the material. Once people see the completed pages they will be eager to look through them over and over again. Keeping pages protected will ensure that photographs and papers will be free from fingerprints and dust as well as acids from handling.

It is important that page protectors be made from polypropylene, polyethylene and polyester plastics. Always avoid any products made from PVC as they will be harmful to photographs.

Events featured in scrapbooks often require more than a double-page spread, so expanding page protectors are a suitable option. These will also allow for more memorabilia to be included in the layouts.

Special pocket pages are available for featuring and protecting memorabilia.

TYPES OF ALBUMS

The most popular album size is 30.5 x 30.5 cm (12 x 12 inches), but smaller sizes are also available. There are three main types of albums: three ringed, strap-hinged and post-bound.

Three-ringed binders are easy to use, hold more pages and are often cheaper than other types of albums. Completed pages are inserted into page protectors that can be easily moved.

Strap-hinged albums allow the book to expand to the length of the strap. Facing pages lie flat, enabling continuity in a double-page spread. The albums usually come with a white background page. Page protectors for these albums can be side-loading or top-loading.

Post-bound albums are expandable, with the addition of extra posts. Pages in post-bound albums can be easily moved around and arranged. Page protectors for these albums are top-loading.

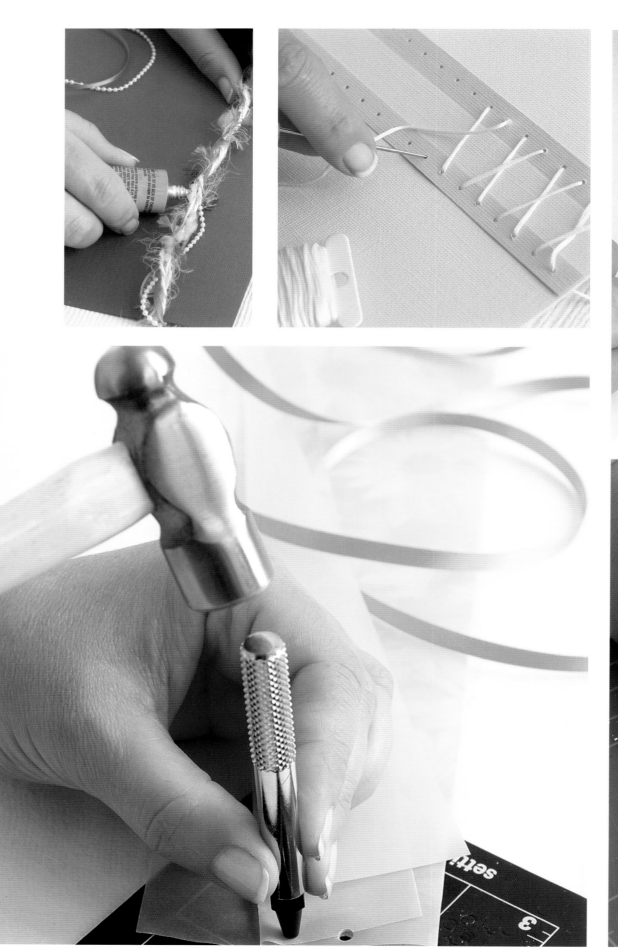

Techniques

Cropping

Cropping is the cutting or trimming of photos to achieve a desired shape, size or effect. Photographs are cropped to highlight the focal point and remove any unnecessary details including those that do not enhance or relate to the overall theme. Cropping equipment ranges from scissors and a pencil to elaborate cutting systems.

CROPPING TIPS

Do not crop one-of-a-kind photographs.

Check each photo's background first. Future generations will be interested in cars, houses, schools, churches etc.

The main shapes used are squares, rectangles, circles and ovals. Other shapes, such as stars and hearts, are great for children's pages.

Too many shapes on one page creates confusion and imbalance and the overall theme will be lost.

WHEN NOT TO CROP

Before you start to crop, consider that limited cropping is often more effective than a busy layout that has too many trimmed shapes. Sometimes framing can be a more suitable option to highlight the focal point.

Never crop one-of-a-kind photographs. If negatives of the photographs are not available, do not crop them.

Do not crop Polaroid photographs. The liquid inside is poisonous and if the photographs have not set properly this liquid will destroy other photographs.

CROPPING TECHNIQUES

Beginners are advised to start with the simplest cropping methods. A paper trimmer is best for cutting straight lines. A template and removable grease pencil (a 'chinagraph' or wax pencil) is good for cutting circles and ovals.

Cutting systems, such as the Coluzzle nested template system, will also cut shapes. However, some cutting systems may take a little getting used to. Since everyone has some bad photographs in their collection, it is recommended that these be used for practice.

1 The decision to crop a photo must first take into account which photo will be the focal point of the layout. Select the shape and size for cropping, remembering to leave details in the background. Line up the square shapes under the paper trimmer. Trim the photograph vertically and horizontally.

2 Simple templates can be used for cropping curved and irregular shapes, as well as rectangles. Place the template over the selected part of the photo and draw around the shape with a grease pencil. Cut the shape out with a sharp pair of scissors. Rub off any bits of grease pencil left behind with a soft cotton cloth.

SPECIAL PUNCHES

A square punch is a quick and easy way to crop out sections of a photograph.

There is a wide range of sizes to choose from. Every scrapbooker should have at least a few different large punches in their collection.

Oval and circle punches are great for cutting those difficult curved lines.

Punches that are designed to crop the corners of photographs are another useful investment for scrapbookers.

3 To use the Coluzzle nested template system, place the photograph on the special backing provided. Position the Coluzzle template over the photo and select the best size for cropping. Cut along the guidelines with the Coluzzle cutter and snip the section remaining on each side with a pair of sharp scissors.

1 Line the photo up on the wrong side of the square punch.

2 Place your hand on the punch and apply even pressure.

Matting

Matting is the process of cutting and placing complementary paper singly or in layers behind a photograph to highlight it. As well as being decorative, matting with acid-free cardstock ensures that photographs are separated from other items on the page.

MATTING TIPS

Cut out the matting with a pair of fancy scissors to create variety.

Using a combination of colours is a great way to highlight photographs.

Varying the width of the matting can produce an interesting visual effect, especially when creating a focal point.

Embellishments, such as eyelets, can also be used on the matting to further draw the eye to the featured photo.

As with cropping, less is sometimes more. There is no need to triple-mat every photo on a layout.

An alternate pattern, such as single, then double, matting can be used to create interest on the page.

CREATING A FOCAL POINT

The matting beneath a photograph needs to be carefully selected so that it does not take the focus away from the photograph. Plain cardstock is the easiest way to achieve highlighting without detracting from the photograph. However, when layering with several mats, printed paper can be used effectively. Try papers that echo colours, patterns or themes in the photo.

Since matting draws attention to the photographs, several layers can be used to create a focal point.

Time is the most **valuable** thing one can spend

–Theophrastus

Scrapbooking Techniques   17

MATTING RECTANGULAR PHOTOGRAPHS

If the photograph is a square or rectangle, adhere it to the corner of the cardstock. Use the markings on the paper trimmer to place the photo and cut the remaining sides at the same distance.

It is not necessary to cut the entire piece of paper. You need only cut to the end of the photo. This saves paper and allows for the matting of other photographs in varying sizes.

If matting more than one colour, repeat this process for each layer.

1 Select pieces of coloured cardstock which match colours in the photograph. When using several layers of matting, make sure the colours work well with each other.

2 Glue the photo to the corner of a piece of cardstock. Use a paper trimmer to line up and cut the matting. Build up the other layers in this way, measuring the size increases with a ruler or paper trimmer.

3 Try varying the widths of the matting to add variety. Tearing the edges of the matting (refer to the section on Paper Tearing) will also add interest. When the layers are complete, adhere the matted photo to the layout.

MATTING CURVED PHOTOGRAPHS

Photographs can be cut into curved shapes by using oval and circle templates and special equipment such as the Coluzzle nested template system. If a cutting system has been used, try selecting the next size up to cut the layers of matting.

An easy-to-use tool called Magic Matter is also great for matting curved photographs. Use it to draw an evenly distanced line around the photo, then cut along the line with a pair of scissors.

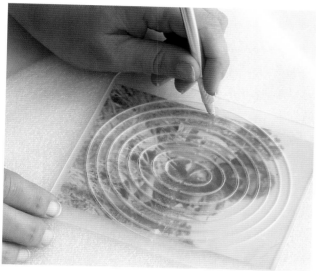

1 Use a template (such as the Coluzzle nested template system) to cut the photograph into an oval shape. The matting can then be cut at the next size up on the template, or cut manually using the Magic Matter system.

2 To use the Magic Matter system glue the oval photograph to the cardstock. Select a Magic Matter disk–the size will determine the width of the matting. Mark the cutting line by moving the Magic Matter disk around the photograph with a graphite pencil.

3 Cut out the matting and rub out any pencil marks with an eraser or a piece of clean cloth. Additional layers of matting of varying widths can be created with the different sizes of Magic Matter disks.

Framing

Frames are not just for photos, they can be used to frame a journalling box, a title, a picture or an entire page. Frames differ from mats as they sit on top of photos, are usually wider and are often embellished. Ready-made frames can be purchased, but knowing how to make a frame to match a scrapbook theme, photograph or design is even better.

BASIC PHOTO FRAMING

Frames can be made from specialty paper, patterned paper or almost any other material, including metal, fabric, foam core and even shrink plastic.

Consider the size of the photo when determining the width of the frame in order to maintain balance.

The frame's inside edge must be slightly smaller than the photo so that the frame completely covers the photo. The outside edge can vary in size, provided it covers the photo.

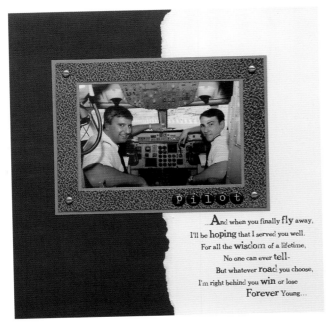

...And when you finally fly away,
I'll be hoping that I served you well.
For all the wisdom of a lifetime,
No one can ever tell-
But whatever road you choose,
I'm right behind you win or lose
Forever Young...

MAKING 3-D FRAMES

Acid-free mat board is a dense, high-quality cardboard used to surround a picture with a wide mat, creating a border between it and the actual frame.

Foam core is similar to cardboard but with a foam inner medium and an outer liner of high-quality paper. Due to its thickness, a foam core frame will sit high above the photo beneath, casting a small shadow inside the cut-out area. This creates a 3-D 'shadow-box' effect that is useful for framing lumpy memorabilia.

EMBELLISHING FRAMES

Frames can be decorated to match the colour, style and mood of a layout.

Wrap the frames in fabric, secured at the back or with ribbons tied in a bow at the front. Stitch corners for rustic flair.

Apply metallic rub-ons to a frame for a rich-looking finish. The use of heat embossing can produce a shiny enamelled finish.

Letters can be stamped onto frames or attached as cut-out letters.

1 Push out the baby frame (see the Template section at the back of this book). Measure the frame and, if required, crop the photo with a paper trimmer. The photo will need to be slightly smaller than the outside edge of the frame.

2 Secure the photo to a mat of white cardstock with glue dots. Add glue dots to the back of the push-out baby frame and attach the frame to the photo.

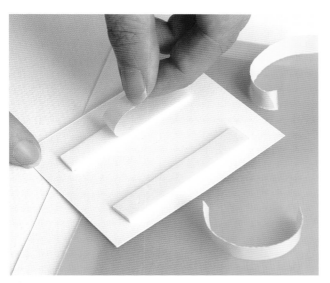

3 Cut out the matted photo frame and stick two strips of Magic Mount to the back of the matting. This will create a raised picture when the matted photo is attached to the layout.

Specialty papers

Specialty papers are those that do not fall under the heading of cardstock or patterned paper. Some of the most prized specialty papers include mulberry, handmade and metallic varieties. They come in a wide array of textures and thicknesses and lend extra interest or add special effects to the pages without greatly increasing the bulk.

MULBERRY AND OTHER SPECIALTY PAPERS

Some of the more common specialty papers are handmade, metallic and mulberry. Vellum is another specialty paper used extensively in scrapbooking; this paper is covered in more detail on page 48

Mulberry is actually a thin, fibrous paper made from the inner bark of the mulberry tree. It is pliable and loosely woven with long fibres. Mulberry paper is often torn to reveal an uneven edge, giving it a soft 'fuzzy' appearance.

There are many other varieties of specialty papers for scrapbooking, including cork, rippled cardboard, maruyama (thin mesh-like Japanese paper), suede and printable canvas. Always ensure the papers are acid and lignin free before using them in an archival album.

HANDMADE PAPERS

Handmade papers add a wonderful texture and homemade feel to a layout. They come in a variety of colours, patterns and thicknesses.

Some handmade papers are made with leaves and flowers embedded in the fibres for a pretty touch, and some are embossed with patterns.

Handmade papers can be easily made by using leftover scraps of cardstock; paper-making kits are available at most craft stores.

METALLIC PAPERS

Papers that give the appearance of metal in a variety of finishes, such as flat, diamond dust, mirror, pearlescent and iridescent, are known as metallic papers.

Colours range from pastels to silver, gold and black. They are often used as photo mats or cut into smaller pieces for faux-metal embellishments such as photo corners.

Inkjet printers and normal inks will not work well on this paper, so if writing on them, use a quick-drying pen such as a Slick Writer.

1 To create a torn-edge effect on matting made from mulberry paper, use a water pen, cotton bud or small paintbrush dipped in water. Draw a line of water along the paper where it is to be torn. This will help to control the tearing.

2 Gently pull the mulberry paper at the wet edges and the fibres will separate easily.

3 Allow the mulberry paper to dry completely before adhering the mat to your layout.

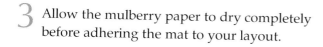

Using vellum

Vellum is a translucent paper similar to, but thicker than, tracing paper. It is acid and lignin free and comes in a variety of colours, printed patterns and textures. Vellum provides many entrancing options for scrapbookers such as subtley patterned backgrounds, delicately layered matting, gorgeous embellishments and translucent pockets.

CHOOSING VELLUM

Vellum takes its name from the medieval paper it resembles that was made from animal skin. Modern vellums are made from plant products and come in a range of colours, patterns and textures.

Select your vellum in conjunction with the background cardstock. Deeper or brighter-coloured backgrounds can be used, as placing the vellum on top will soften or mute the colour dramatically.

If you wish to match the cardstock to a photograph, a layer of white vellum on top will mute the cardstock, providing a closer match to the photograph.

Vellum is the ideal choice for making delicate pockets on your scrapbook pages. The translucent quality of the vellum lends elegance to the page while still providing practical storage for memorabilia.

JOURNALLING WITH VELLUM

Vellum can make your journalling easier. In the back of this book you have been given templates for writing fonts. Simply place vellum over the top and trace with your archivally safe pen, then add colour.

Vellum can even be used with a computer printer to great effect. With some printers it helps to use a colour other than black, such as grey, brown or blue, to eliminate the bleeding process.

Print out headings or text on a sheet of paper (A4). This will show exactly where the text will be printed.

Use a removable adhesive to attach a scrap piece of vellum on top of the writing, then refeed the paper through the printer. This is an attractive, economical method for using up scrap pieces of vellum. See the Using Computers section for more ideas.

ATTACHING VELLUM

Vellum is translucent so most adhesives will show through. However, different techniques can be used to avoid this problem.

If using vellum to mat photographs, start attaching the layers from the top. Any adhesive can be used underneath the photograph without being noticed.

If nothing is being placed on top of the vellum, there are several suitable adhesive products. These include clear-mounting tabs, double-sided tapes and vellum adhesive sprays. The least noticeable is the vellum adhesive spray, which allows the flexibility of repositioning. Access to a Xyron machine provides a big advantage as this machine can transform a piece of vellum into a sticker.

Scrapbook stores also carry a large range of brads, eyelets, snaps, paper nails and conchos that are effective when mounting vellum onto cardstock.

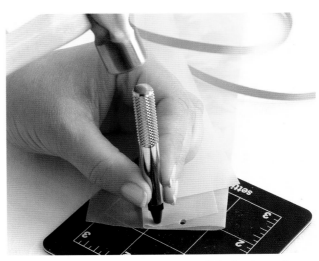

1 Cut out two rectangles of vellum to to make a pocket for your layout. Fold each piece in half then make a flap by folding at an angle as shown. The second piece should have a larger flap. Slot the two pieces together.

2 Punch three sets of two small holes into the vellum with a hole punch and hammer.

3 Secure the vellum with two pieces of matching ribbon. Thread each ribbon through the holes and tie it in a knot. Embellish the pocket as desired.

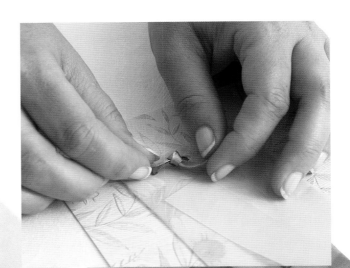

Cutting

Cutting techniques are an essential part of scrapbook creation. Cutting creates the shapes and titles that are integral to the layout's design. Cutting equipment ranges from a humble pair of paper scissors to the deckle-edge or fancy varieties. Precut push-out shapes are also available, as well as sophisticated die-cutting machinery.

USING DIE-CUT SHAPES

Die-cut shapes can be quick and effective embellishments for a layout. They can be layered with other colours to give them dimension or chalked to make them appear more realistic.

Die-cut shapes serve several useful functions. They can be used for journalling and for adding dates, locations, and names.

Die-cuts can hide personal journalling that is not meant for everyone's viewing.

Die-cuts can also create interesting backgrounds for a layout.

Scrapbook stores sell manufactured die-cuts that come in a large assortment of themes and phrases. They can be easily personalized and adapted to the style and colours of your layouts. Embellishment techniques (featured in the picture) include decorating with chalks, rubber stamps, printed papers and sequins.

DIE-CUTTING MACHINES

Scrapbook stores often provide access to expensive die-cutting machines. These machines can cut through cardstock, foam, fabric, printed paper or photographs. It is recommended that no more than four layers be cut at one time, less when using heavier cardstock.

Die-cut letters can create a quick and easy title or heading for any layout. Letters can be aged or softened with chalks or highlighted with gel pens. A shadow effect can be easily created by cutting out the same letter in two different colours. The letters can then be overlapped, allowing the bottom colour to show through. Experiment with revealing the bottom letter on the bottom right or left or top right or left. Stick the letters together, then apply them to the layout.

Try to use leftover scraps for cutting out letters to minimize waste.

SCISSORS

Fancy scissors can be purchased in a range of styles. Use fancy scissors to add flair to photograph matting or journalling blocks. When matting a photograph, try to vary the overall look by layering a fancy edge in between two straight-edged mats.

When cutting a square or rectangular shape with fancy scissors it is important to cut the mat slightly larger (about one extra centimetre or ¼ inch) than required. Turn the paper over and draw lines with a ruler and pencil about 4 mm (⅛ inch) from the edge. Use this line as a cutting guide. The longest points on the scissors' blade

should always land on the edge of the line. This will help to maintain the correct shape. This technique also works when you are cutting circles or ovals. Use a template on the reverse side of the paper to draw guidelines, then begin cutting.

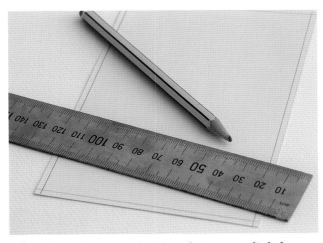

1 Cut the paper for the photo mat slightly larger (about one extra centimetre or ¼ inch) than required. Turn the paper over and draw lines with a ruler and pencil no more than 4 mm (⅛ inch) from the edge.

2 Using the pencil line as a guide, begin cutting with the deckle-edged scissors. The tip of the furthest point should touch the line. Continue cutting all the sides in the same manner.

3 Turn the photo mat over. To make a more decorative edging, use chalks to highlight the deckled edges. Glue the mat to the photo.

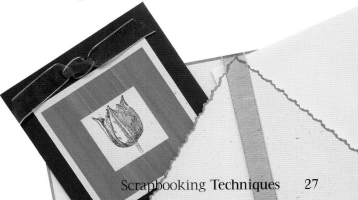

Paper tearing and crumpling

Tearing or ripping paper instead of cutting it with scissors can add definition, texture or softness to a page, depending on its application. Paper crumpling, also known as scrunching or wrinkling, is another great way to achieve a textured look without making the layout too 'lumpy'.

TEARING TIPS

Some other popular effects achieved by using torn paper are:

Natural elements such as water, dirt, sand, trees and leaves, grass, mountains and the sky

Teddy bears, cats, dogs (anything that has fur)

Woollen items or things that are fuzzy

Flowers

TEARING PAPER

Paper is made from compressed fibres, and tearing it breaks those fibres apart. Each type of paper will offer different effects when torn and some papers are easier to tear than others.

Straight edges can sometimes create a harsh impression that detracts from the overall appearance of layout designs. This is especially true when overlapping two or more layers of paper. Tearing the graduated edges will soften the look by removing harsh lines and corners. The eye is immediately directed to the focus, which is usually the photograph.

Many papers have a white reverse side. After tearing the paper in two, one piece will reveal a white edge while the other piece will show none. Torn pieces that reveal a white edge will provide extra definition on a page. For a softer look, tear paper dyed through and through to reveal a less stark contrast.

TEARING TECHNIQUES

The tearing process is simple; hold one side of the paper still, and use the other hand to slowly tear toward the body.

At first, tearing might be made easier by drawing a light guideline with a pencil on the reverse side of the paper. However, tearing looks great when it has a free-flowing effect and it is not necessarily confined to the boundaries of a line. Paper looks even more effective when it is torn in a jagged, uneven or sloping line.

If tearing small pieces, use a small, controlled tearing motion. For larger pieces, tear in one smooth movement. Experiment with tearing effects on different types of papers.

Journalling boxes, page titles and photos can look effective with torn edges. However, use copies of photos rather than tearing the originals.

PAPER CRUMPLING

Paper crumpling adds texture to the page without being too prominent. Combining the same papers on a layout –but with one crumpled and one left plain–can create an interesting background without the addition of new colours.

Crumpling paper is very easy. It can be done in two ways: dry crumpling and wet crumpling.

For the dry method, just crumple the paper by hand and then unfold and smooth it out. To obtain more wrinkles, repeat the process until the desired effect is achieved.

For wet crumpling, follow the easy step-by-step instructions. This method works best with card-stock, as most patterned papers will disintegrate when wet.

1 Hold the cardstock under gentle running water until wet, or use a spray bottle filled with water to spray the cardstock until it is completely damp.

2 Crumple the cardstock into a ball with your hands. Carefully open your hands to see the creases made and repeat the crumpling if desired. If a small hole should appear, don't worry–this will add to the shabby look.

3 For a rumpled, uneven look, leave the paper to dry naturally. To achieve a flat but still wrinkled effect iron the cardstock while wet or dry, setting the steam option to 'off'. The end result will resemble handmade paper.

Paper rolling and scraping

Paper rolling adds yet another interesting dimension to the edges of torn paper and is especially effective when applied to photograph mats and title boxes. Paper rolling is great for producing the 'shabby' or 'worn' look often used in heritage layouts. Paper-scraping techniques will also help to achieve an aged appearance.

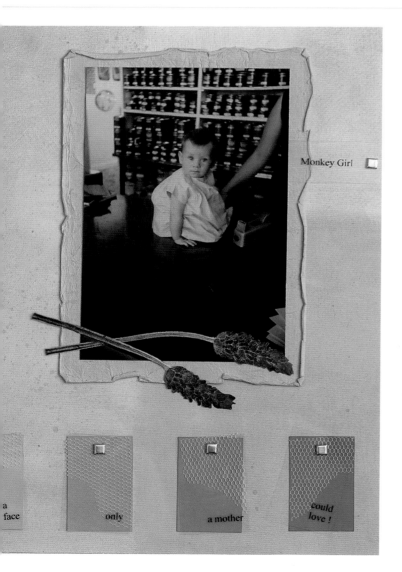

PAPER ROLLING

Paper rolling refers to the rolling of a torn edge of paper between the fingertips until it holds itself in a rolled or curled position.

Rolled sections of paper can vary in size and tightness of roll; there are no specific rules on how the roll should look.

Different types of paper will give slightly different effects, but the best papers to use are cardstock or printed paper. Vellum and most other specialty or handmade papers do not roll well.

Space cuts along the paper's edge at uneven intervals, and make sure they do not extend too far into the paper, about 1 cm ($^1/_4$ inch). The deeper the cut, the wider the rolled edge.

Some practice may be needed at first to get the rolling action just right. Too much rolling may tear or pill the paper, and too little may cause it to unravel.

ROLLING IDEAS

Once a level of confidence is reached in this technique there are many options for its use. Tear a hole in the middle of a piece of paper and roll the edges from the inside towards the outside, then place a photo or journalling box behind the paper so it 'peeks' through the hole.

Layer several pieces of rolled paper on top of each other and space them slightly apart so each rolled edge can be seen. Try a beach theme layout with several different shades of blue cardstock to create the effect of waves.

Roll the edges of photo mats and sit the photo inside the rolls. Roll one or more edges of journalling boxes or titles.

Colour or gild the reverse side of the paper before rolling it, so the rolled edges will be a contrasting colour and the rolling technique is accentuated.

1 Tear the edge of the paper. Turn the paper over and colour the edge with metallic rub-ons. Cut small nicks along the torn edge with scissors at different angles. This helps set the direction of each section so that the finished rolls will sit at different angles to each other.

2 For thick paper, wet the torn edge to make it more pliable. Place the paper face up on a work surface. Using an index finger, lift and roll each cut section toward the centre of the paper. Roll the edge gently backwards and forwards until the desired curl is created.

3 Roll one edge on each of several large pieces of paper and overlap to create an interesting background for the page. Colour with metallic rub-ons or chalks to further accentuate the rolling technique.

PAPER SCRAPING

Paper scraping will only work with cardstock, as paper is not thick enough.

The best method for scraping paper is to hold a piece of cardstock in one hand, with the edges lying straight out in front of you, so the cardstock is horizontal to the floor.

Using one of the blades on a pair of sharp scissors, scrape down the edge of the cardstock, starting at the point furthest away from you and bringing the scissors toward you.

Repeat this over and over until the cardstock starts to become a little 'fluffy' at the edges.

Wipe off the fluff and the result should be similar to the edges of the pages of an old book.

This process is also known as 'knocking' the edges and works very well with vintage-style layouts.

Great Grandmother

Chalking

Chalking is a technique used to give extra colour, dimension or softness to items on scrapbook layouts. It is applied effectively for an aged or distressed look, especially with heritage and 'vintage-look' designs. A small investment in a box of acid-free chalks will provide many options for decorating papers and embellishments.

CHALKING TIPS

Choose a chalk colour one or two shades darker than the item to be chalked for definition.

Test on pieces of scrap paper until you get the right amount of colour.

Apply chalk in a circular motion for larger areas, and in a side-to-side motion for edges and thin lines.

Excess chalk or chalk dust should be tapped off the paper, rather than rubbed or flicked away.

Experiment with blending different chalk colours. Always apply lighter colours first then gradually add darker colours in layers, blending the edges with each added layer.

Add definition to the edges of chalked images with acid-free pens or pencils in co-ordinating colours.

Create negative space images by holding a cut-out shape on paper, then chalking around the edges in a light circular motion. Lift the cut-out shape up and its outline will be left on the paper, surrounded by a soft frame of chalk.

CHALKING EQUIPMENT

An assortment of applicators will provide added flexibility when chalking. Use a cotton wool ball for large areas, or a narrow-tipped applicator for smaller areas, fine lines or edges.

Most applicators are inexpensive and can be purchased at local supermarkets. Cotton swabs or balls are good for this, as are sponge-tipped applicators (similar to eye make-up applicators). There are also special chalk applica-

tors available which have an alligator clip to hold small cotton pompoms. Often, a small fine-tip brush will come in handy for detailed projects and when chalking embossed suede paper.

The only other tool required is an eraser to quickly repair any mistakes. A kneaded rubber eraser manufactured by Design is available at many craft or art supply stores. It will completely remove any chalk from the paper.

APPLYING CHALKS

Always cover your work area with a large piece of paper or cloth. Choose an appropriate applicator and lightly rub it over the chalk. It is better to apply the chalk lightly and add more in layers.

Using a small circular motion, lightly rub the applicator over the area to be chalked. Add more chalk to the applicator as needed, a little at a time. Continue to apply and blend layers of chalk until the desired effect is achieved.

Anthony

SEALING CHALKS

There is no need to seal chalked items with fixatives for most applications. Left alone, they will completely set within 24 hours. If a large area has been heavily chalked, turn it onto a piece of scrap paper and rub the back firmly with your hand. This will speed up the setting process by compressing the chalk into the paper fibres.

SOFTENING EFFECTS

Whites or ivories can look too stark next to other items on a page. Try softening them with a light application of chalk to give a pale pastel finish. Lightly apply chalk to the raised edges of embossed paper to extend the colour scheme. Sand edges of patterned paper or photos to reveal some of the white paper inside, then chalk the white areas.

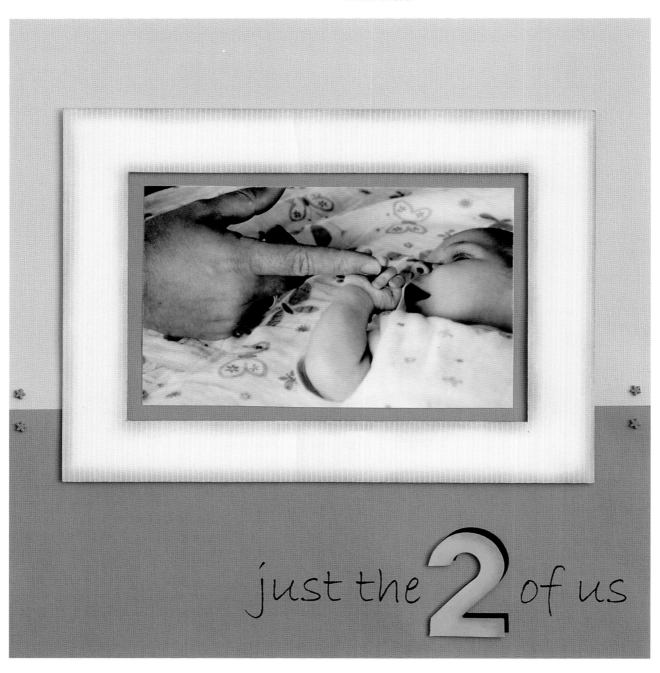

AGEING EFFECTS

Age or 'distress' items using a blend of brown, grey and black chalks. Chalk the edge of torn paper for extra dimension.

1 Select a textured paper for a photo frame such as this corrugated paper. Mark the photo measurements on the back with pencil and cut out with a paper trimmer.

USING STENCILS

Use stencils to apply chalked images. Dab over the open area with a chalked cotton wool ball to leave an image. Clean up untidy edges with an eraser.

2 Select a darker-coloured chalk that will blend with your layout while creating a 'three-dimensional' effect. Shade the inner and outer edge of the frame with a sponge-tip chalk applicator.

3 Use the numeral stencil or a die-cut numeral and shade the edge with the same-coloured chalk. Leave the chalked elements to set for 24 hours before attaching them to your page.

Punching

Punches are versatile, easy to use and come in hundreds of different shapes and styles. On layouts, punched shapes can be used to create embellishments, interesting backgrounds and photo corners. Punched images can also be combined to create eye-catching decorations with minimal effort.

PUNCHING TIPS

Turn the punch over before punching out an image so the image is visible. This will help prevent wasting paper as the spacing between punches can be controlled.

With repeated use the punch may become dull. Punch through some aluminium foil or the finest grade of sandpaper to sharpen the metal cutting mechanism.

If the cutting mechanism is sticking, punch using some wax paper. This will lubricate the punch and eliminate any sticking.

PUNCHED SHAPES

Punches can be purchased in varying sizes of one particular shape. The most popular shape is the square punch with the circle coming in a close second. These punches can be used to create borders, headings and embellishments. They are also used to crop photos.

Other punches on the market will create decorative corners. The most basic one rolls the edges, others punch out a more elegant design.

A hole punch and hammer are essential for punching small round holes for eyelets (refer to the Using Vellum and Using Metals sections for more details).

Punching is a resourceful way to use up any scrap paper. Whole layouts can be punched with very little paper. Use printed as well as solid papers for punching projects. The printed papers add interest and a new dimension to punched projects.

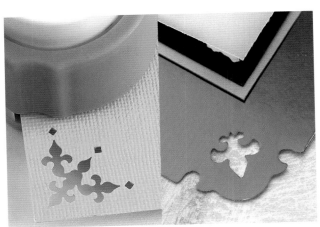

PUNCHED PATTERNS

Both the punched-out shapes and the holes they leave behind have a decorative potential; (see the Alfred Buckley layout overleaf).

The possibilities of punched shapes are further increased by cutting them in half, either across or diagonally.

The shape produced by the square punch is often cut diagonally to form a right triangle. This can, for example, become the basis of a quilting pattern.

Punched shapes can be put together to form a pattern such as the attractive fleur-de-lis punched shapes that form the bridal flower motifs (pictured) in The Bride layout.

Punched shapes can also be chalked, highlighted with pens or mounted, using Magic Mount for a three-dimensional effect. Extra touches include gilding, sequins and diamantés.

PUNCHING TECHNIQUES

The easiest way to punch is to turn the punch over, slide a piece of paper into the punch and press down with the heel of the hand.

A Punch Mate can be used to complete projects that require a lot of punching. It has a lever that minimizes the effort needed to punch a shape.

Since punches are a precision cutting tool they require some care to maximize their lifespan. They may be used on 80 gsm to 230 gsm (3 oz to 8 oz) paper, depending on the type of punch.

Manufacturers do not recommend that punches be used on light paper or uneven cardstock as they could cause the punch to jam.

Store punches in a dry environment to prevent corrosion. If a punch becomes corroded, a dab of light oil should remove it. Remember to remove any excess oil before reusing the punch.

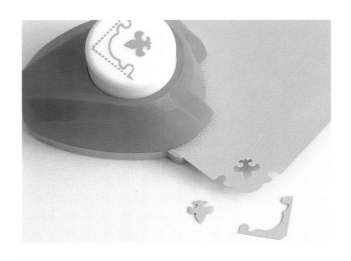

1 Use green paper for punching out the leaf shapes. Slide the green paper into the punch and press down. Repeat this, working along the edge of the paper to avoid waste. Punch out small daisy shapes from the white paper.

2 Use a larger daisy punch to make shapes from the remaining white paper. Punch out the flower centres using a small dot or tiny flower punch and yellow paper. Punch enough shapes for about ten flowers and five leaves.

3 Use tweezers and silicone glue to create the three-dimensional effect flowers. Glue two layers of daisy shapes together, then glue the yellow centre on the top. Glue the daisies to leaf shapes if desired, then attach to the page or card.

Alfred Buckley - My Great Grandfather

PETER & KAY
1st Nov 1942

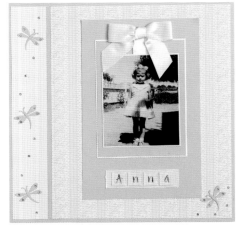

Anna

Rubber stamping and wet embossing

Rubber stamping and wet embossing were around long before archival scrapbooking came on the scene. Scrapbookers now use these techniques to create distinctive backgrounds, titles and embellishments. With some knowledge and a dash of inspiration, the scrapbooker can bring a unique dimension to any layout.

RUBBER STAMPING AND EMBOSSING

In the past, keen 'stampers' confined their craft mainly to cards and papercraft. However, as scrapbookers are always seeking new innovations for layouts, rubber stamping and embossing are now a feature in many scrapbook albums.

The layouts in this section have all been enhanced with a rubber stamping or embossing technique. These techniques take little time, but are very effective.

Experiment with different techniques and do not be afraid to try new things. Make each layout a work of art by incorporating different media.

However, before adding rubber stamping and embossing to cherished layouts a scrapbooker must become knowledgeable about the different stamp pads and their uses.

DYE INK PADS

Dye ink pads are water based and dry quickly on all types of paper.

These pads are acid free, permanent and sometimes waterproof, if indicated on the cover.

Dye ink pads come in a large assortment of colours. However, as the dye ink dries it becomes lighter and slightly muted.

It is recommended that scrapbookers purchase brands that are labelled archival, since archival inks are not only acid free, but fade resistant as well.

Dye ink pads are not used for wet embossing. However, they can be applied directly on paper to create a beautiful multicoloured background.

Use light-coloured dye ink pads with shadow stamps to create subtle backgrounds for titles, headings, adornments or journalling blocks.

PIGMENT INK PADS

Pigment ink pads produce sharp and striking impressions. They provide rich, saturated colours that work well with embossing.

Pigment inks come in a wide range of colours and are acid free and fade resistant. It is recommended that clear embossing powder be used with pigment inks. However, a pigment ink can be applied without embossing as long as it is given adequate drying time.

Since pigment inks are made from particles of pigment, they work best on non-glossy paper, especially in the absence of embossing powder.

Drying time may vary, especially with metallic inks, so a heat gun may be used to set the colour. Simply hold the heat gun above the impressions and move it along in an even manner. This will help the colour set into the paper.

SPECIALTY INK PADS

Metallic inks are pigment inks that often require heat setting. They offer more vibrancy and pearlescence than the standard pigment pad. However, many of these pads are not child safe and some are not archival or acid free.

Recently, metallic inks that work well on all types of media and do not require heat have appeared on the market. Check labels carefully for details.

Specialty pads, such as VersaMark, provide a watermark effect on paper (see the step-by-step instructions). These create wonderful backgrounds and can be used in conjunction with chalks and Pearl Ex products.

A new product called StazOn ink can be used on a large range of surfaces like plastic, metal, glass, ceramic, laminated paper, coated paper and leather. It is a fast-drying, solvent ink that provides flexibility when creating works of art.

EMBOSSING PADS

Embossing pads can be clear or have a slight tint that makes it easier to see an impression's placement before applying the embossing powder.

These pads are used only for wet embossing. Once applied on paper, embossing powder must be added, then heated to create a beautiful raised image.

Embossing powders come in a large assortment of colours and a few textures. Images with fine details usually require fine embossing powder for a crisp image. However, not all rubber stamps are suitable for wet embossing. Suitability is determined by the texture, grain and detail of the rubber stamps.

Often rubber stamps created from images of photographs can only be used with dye-based ink and some pigment ink pads. It is suggested that some time be spent experimenting before deciding on the best ink pad for a rubber stamp.

1 Choose a simple stamp to form an effective background pattern on solid green cardstock. Ink the stamp with a watermark ink pad such as VersaMark.

2 Stamp the image onto the paper. The colour of the paper will be slightly darkened, creating an eye-catching background.

3 Repeat this process until a cascading pattern is achieved. Leave the background to dry completely before assembling the layout.

EMBOSSING TOOLS

Embossing pens are an invaluable addition for any scrapbooker.

Embossing pens can be purchased in an assortment of nib styles and offer the scrapbooker the ability to emboss their own handwriting. These pens are used in conjunction with embossing powders and a heat tool.

When using wet embossing, a heat tool is the best source of heat to set the image.

The heat from a heat tool is extremely hot and, unlike a blow-dryer that blows air, it produces a direct heat that melts and sets the embossing powder.

The heat tools can be purchased in a range of styles and sizes.

Heat guns can also be used to shrink plastic that has been stamped or embossed. Read the manufacturer's directions before beginning.

WET EMBOSSING

Wet embossing can transform an ordinary die-cut into a work of art.

In the layout Precious Little One, an ordinary blue die-cut was selected. Colour was added directly to the die-cut from a pigment-based pad. Next, clear embossing powder was applied and set with a heat tool. The process was repeated until just the right look was achieved.

The wet embossing process adds dimension to the die-cut and will naturally create a crackled effect, especially when the process is repeated a number of times.

Plain stickers can be revitalized by applying the embossing ink and then sprinkling clear embossing powder over the image. However, in this instance, the heat tool must be used with caution, since many new stickers are plastic based.

EMBOSSING POWDERS

Embossing powders are available in a wide range of colours. They are to be used in conjunction with an embossing ink pad.

Simply ink the stamp with embossing ink and stamp the image on to the paper. Next, sprinkle on the desired embossing powder colour. Tap off the excess embossing powder. Use the heat gun to set the powder.

Once set, the image will appear raised and bolder in colour. The layout entitled Belinda shows an example of this technique. The flowers were embossed on coloured paper with white embossing powder.

Printed papers work well with the embosssing powder process and provide a more artistic feel.

ALPHABET STAMPING TIPS

Alphabet sets come in different sizes and styles and can be used with every type of ink pad.

Use a set of alphabet stamps for titles, tags and other embellishments.

Use a negative alphabet stamp for eye-catching titles.

Stamp letters onto a strip of paper and then cut them out for a more interesting tiled effect.

Creating titles

A title is an important element of a page. It tells the reader who the page is about or what event is being featured. It can set the mood of the page as the scrapbooker can select the colours and fonts that suit each layout. The title may be dignified and formal for a heritage or wedding layout, or hip and bright for a layout about children.

IDEAS FOR TITLES

The inspiration for a title might be immediate or it might require some thought. Often, the inspiration can be taken from magazines, ads, cards, books, poems, quotes or song lyrics. Ideas can also be sparked by the photographs.

The title may be large and part of the focal point or it may be smaller and subtle, complementing the photographs.

Titles can be hand-drawn or created by using alphabet stickers, alphabet templates, letter tiles, stamps, alphabet beads, computer generated fonts, die-cut letters or ready-made add-ons.

The title can be embellished with coloured pencils, chalks, embossing inks and powders, beads, buttons, eyelets, brads, ribbon, raffia and other small notions.

LETTERING STENCILS AND COMPUTERS

Lettering stencils come in a range of different fonts. To use the stencil in the Template section of this book, turn it over and trace each letter with a pencil on to the back of a sheet of paper. Cut out with a pair of scissors. This method avoids any erasing. However, some printed papers need to be face up to ensure appropriate use of the pattern. A vanishing-ink pen or a soft pencil (refer to the step-by-step section on page 75) is used when working with the stencil face up.

The computer is a fantastic tool when a quick, impressive title is needed to complete a layout. Titles can be created using computer fonts downloaded from the internet. On the Soulmate layout the title has been printed onto a piece of cardstock then hand-cut with a craft knife. A good pair of craft scissors can be used to cut titles printed onto cardstock.

TITLE EMBELLISHMENTS

A title can be created or embellished with notions, metals and chalks to add character and appeal.

The heading A Day Spent with Friendson page 74 shows two different techniques. The first part was created from a computer font. The second part, Friends, was made by hand. Each letter was traced onto cardstock using a stencil. Depth was created by adding a darker background and embellishments (refer to the step-by-step instructions for more details).

Eye-catching titles can be created from photographs, as shown in the layout entitled Decker.

Photographs of nature-based images such as sea, sand or foliage make very effective stencilled titles.

Think twice before discarding any poor photos or cropped leftovers. Unwanted pieces can easily be transformed into special titles.

A Day Spent with FRIENDS

We packed a picnic lunch and headed off to the park. The kids had a ball playing in the leaves.   May 20th, 2001

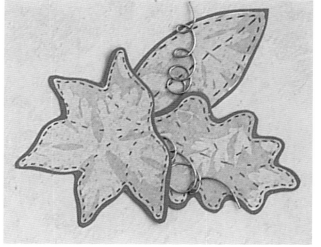

1 Remove the uppercase lettering stencil from the back of the book (see the Template section). Trace each letter onto a sheet of printed paper with a soft pencil or vanishing ink pen. Cut out with scissors and remove any pencil marks with an eraser.

2 Adhere the letter to plain cardstock to create the matting. Use a ruler or a Magic Matter disk to create the guidelines around the letter. Cut out with a scalpel or sharp pair of scissors.

3 Embellish the letter as desired. In this case, pen stroke 'stitching' was created by marking the edge of the printed paper layer with dashes to add a handmade look.

Using pens

Pens and markers are among the most common and versatile supplies that a scrapbooker can purchase. They are made in a large assortment of nibs, colours and sizes. With some practice and imagination scrapbookers can use pens and markers to create a wide variety of lettering that will bring character to a layout.

PEN TIPS

Store pens flat to prevent ink flooding to the tips.

Avoid exposing the pens to air for long periods of time as this dries out the tips, making writing less even.

Do practise pen work on scraps of actual paper from layouts so you get a good idea of colouring, bleed, etc.

As each pen nib produces a different result, try mixing a few together when creating titles, captions or journalling.

If using watercolours with pen work, use pens that are labelled 'permanent' so the pen ink will not run when wet.

Outline the shape of a letter with a monoline pen, then apply chalks or watercolours within the outline.

Gel pens can be used on both light and dark paper.

PEN TYPES

So many types of pens are available to scrapbookers that it is best to start off with the basic nib-styles and spend some time working with each of them.

The four basic nibs are monoline, chisel, scroll and brush. Many pens on the market have dual tips, one on each end. The nibs usually vary in size or style.

Since pens are permanent, create a rough draft before attempting to write on the actual layout. Draw light pencil lines on the pages to help regulate spacing and size. Once the lettering is complete and the ink has dried, rub out the guidelines with an art rubber.

Some advanced pen techniques, such as chisel pen lettering, may require extensive practice. Consider taking a beginner's calligraphy class or purchasing a step-by-step study guide available from bookstores.

MONOLINE PENS

Monoline pens are the most commonly used among scrapbookers. They have a round tapered edge and produce a continuous line, with no deviation in thickness. The monoline pens can be purchased in a range of sizes from ultra-thin to thick. They are ideal for creating titles, borders, captions, journalling or adding embellishments.

BRUSH NIBS

The brush nib is quite similar to an artist's paintbrush. It produces a whimsical effect that will enhance any layout. The brush nib, unlike the monoline, will vary in thickness, depending on the amount of pressure applied when writing. Try using the brush nib on its side rather than the tip. A heavier, wider stroke should be used on the downstroke, and a much lighter touch on the upstroke.

CHISEL-TIP AND SCROLL-TIP PENS

The chisel-tip pen is slightly more difficult to use. Produce broad and narrow strokes by holding the nib at a 45-degree angle. Movement should be perpendicular to the body, keeping the pen at the same angle. Letters will be formed parallel to the sides of a page rather than with a slant or slope.

The scroll-tip pen is similar but has a notch placed directly in the middle. This added feature produces a double line when writing. Use these pens to border journal entries, title boxes or captions.

GEL PENS

Gel pens are another favourite of avid scrap-bookers but only use those that are of archival quality and acid free. They come in a large assortment of colours and features, such as glitter, milky, metallic, pastel and fluorescent finishes.

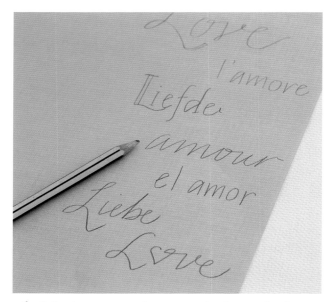

1 Select papers and prepare the layout background. Then use a soft lead pen to write the words on the paper.

2 Trace over the words with different pen nibs to create a varied look. This layout uses monoline and chisel-tip pens.

3 Erase any noticeable pencil lines with an eraser, being careful not to press too hard. Attach remaining items to complete the layout.

Using computers

Computers can be one of the best resources for scrapbookers. Many font programs for scrapbookers are available on CD-ROM or can be downloaded from the internet. Scanners used in conjunction with a computer can create altered and enhanced images and are valuable for duplicating and storing precious layouts.

FONT PRINTING TIPS

Always use acid-free computer-compatible papers. Check the printer settings (under 'media type') to achieve the best results.

Use leftover scraps of printed paper. Create a text box the same size as your scrap of paper and add journalling to fit. Print a test copy on plain paper, then temporarily attach the scrap in position with Hermafix. Run the paper through the printer, then detach your scrap.

Print the text in a light-grey colour and trace over with pens for a perfect but 'hand-done' look.

Printers vary so take time to read the instruction manual.

If printing directly on coated papers, such as vellum, allow plenty of time for the ink to dry.

COMPUTER FONTS

Often scrapbookers dislike the look of their handwriting and feel that it will detract from their layouts. If this is the case, experiment with a word-processing package such as Microsoft Word.

The benefits of computer fonts are obvious– layouts look neater and more journalling will fit into allocated spaces.

Computer text can appear impersonal but this does not have to be the case. Many beautiful fonts are available, including 'hand-written fonts', that look great and match the style of any layout.

Experimenting with fonts can be fun, especially when creating vertical titles, reversed-out titles and mixing fonts within a title. The appearance of the most basic fonts already included in word-processing packages can be varied by changing the size of the letters, selecting bold and italics or varying the spacing between letters.

FONTS FOR SCRAPBOOKS

For serious scrapbookers, special software packages (such as Lettering Delights, Creating Lettering by Creating Keepsakes, and HugWare by ProvoCraft) provide a selection of fonts and tools to add colour and pattern within the fonts.

Acquiring new fonts is easy, provided you learn about the font management system on your computer before installing the file. Most fonts come packaged in ZIP files which must be decompressed before installation.

An enormous variety of fonts can be downloaded for free from the internet. However, up-to-date virus protection is essential. Scrapbook magazines often name the fonts used in projects and this is a great way to identify attractive fonts to download. Use a good search engine, such as Google, to locate 'free font' sites, then download the desired fonts to a disk or your desktop for installation.

SCANNING

Scanners are similar to cameras, in that they're used to capture images. They can be useful for cropping and enlarging photographs, or copying memorabilia like artworks, old packaging, old fabrics, handwriting and family heirlooms, such as jewellery.

Items such as paper clips, string or even cereal can be placed directly onto the scanner to create interesting titles.

Scanners are useful for adjusting poor-quality photos by cropping out unwanted details. Experienced computer users can improve copies of heritage photos using the scanner and computer programs such as Adobe Photoshop.

A great idea for scrapbookers is to scan albums and store them on CD-ROMs. They can be duplicated easily as gifts for family and friends. It is also a good idea to store a copy of the CD-ROM in a safe or firebox.

1 Insert two text boxes with appropriate measurements to fit the layout. Choose different fonts for each box. Narrow the first text box so only one letter appears on each line. If two letters appear, simply add a space. Print a test-copy on plain paper.

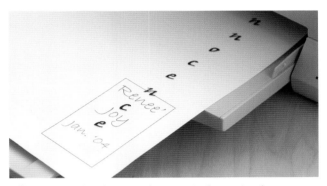

2 Add a shadow to the vertical text in the narrow box. Select the text box and eliminate the black outline (using the Format Text menu). For the second text box, use horizontal print that has been centred. Change the text colour to match your layout and print a test copy.

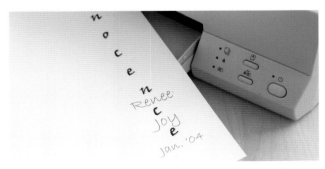

3 Ensure the two text boxes are positioned correctly. Select the second text box and eliminate the black outline. Print a test copy before printing onto cardstock (A4). If using a long piece of cardstock, make the adjustment on the page setup to reflect its actual length.

Using stickers

Stickers are a quick and easy way to embellish a scrapbook layout. They are available in thousands of themes, styles and colours, including very useful alphabet and numeral stickers. With some creativity, stickers can be decorated and positioned so that they add life and movement to the scrapbook page.

STICKER TIPS

Any leftover stickers can be used to create birthday cards, invitations and gift tags.

Try mixing alphabet sticker fonts to create a whimsical look on a layout.

Customize your stickers to reflect the overall style of the layout. Experiment with sanding and dimensional magic.

Use tweezers to help position stickers with ease.

WORKING WITH STICKERS

All stickers used in an album must be acid and lignin free. If not, the acid in the stickers will migrate to the surrounding papers and photographs. Check for 'acid-free' on the label when you purchase stickers.

When working with stickers, try to group them together to create a scene. Anchoring stickers will create interest and depth in a layout. They must have purpose and meaning on the page so they can enhance the theme. Remember to always keep a layout balanced. This includes the positioning of stickers.

If using only one sticker on a sheet, cut around the sticker and experiment with its position before attaching it to the layout. This will ensure a pleasing result in the end.

CUSTOMIZING STICKERS

Raising stickers will enhance realism and create a three-dimensional look. This can be done with Magic Mount, a type of three-dimensional adhesive. The layout entitled A Day at the Zoo on page 84 demonstrates this technique. The stickers appear to be jumping off the page, giving them a whimsical feel.

Stickers can be customized by applying other techniques such as tearing and chalking.

If some of the stickers on a sheet are not used they will still make fabulous embellishments for other papercraft projects such as cards and bookmarks.

ALPHABET STICKERS

When using alphabet stickers there is a sure-fire method for getting them straight, centred and in the correct position on a layout.

Simply use the top edge of the sticker sheet, placing approximately one-third of each letter on the top and allowing the remainder to hang off.

Once the word or phrase has been spelt out and spaced, take the sheet to the layout and attach the letters in the predetermined location. Peel the sheet away from the bottom third of the letters and stick this portion down.

If a sticker is accidentally placed in the wrong spot or does not work in the overall appearance of the layout, use a bottle of Un-Du to remove it.

Daniel, Lachlan and Andrew are standing,
Then in front is Fletcher, Spencer,
Caitlin, Elizabeth and Kaitlyn

1 Always select acid-free stickers. Check their positioning on the layout. Cut off narrow strips of Magic Mount (try 2.5 cm or 1 inch wide) with a sharp pair of scissors.

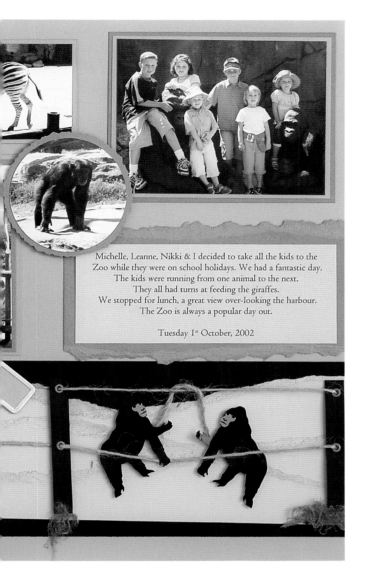

Michelle, Leanne, Nikki & I decided to take all the kids to the
Zoo while they were on school holidays. We had a fantastic day.
The kids were running from one animal to the next.
They all had turns at feeding the giraffes.
We stopped for lunch, a great view over-looking the harbour.
The Zoo is always a popular day out.

Tuesday 1st October, 2002

2 Cut off small sections from the strip of Magic Mount and arrange them on the sticky side (back) of the sticker. Add enough pieces so all parts of the sticker, such as the giraffe's neck, will be supported when raised.

3 Sprinkle talcum powder over the sticker to nullify the stickiness of the sticker back. When complete, peel off the backing to expose the adhesive side of the Magic Mount. Attach the sticker to your layout.

Using notions

What are notions? They are items of haberdashery that personalize scrapbook pages and add interest. Notions are not exclusive to scrapbooking and can be purchased in sewing supply and haberdashery stores. Notions can add the perfect finishing touch to a layout; choosing what to use and how to use it is all part of the fun of this hobby.

TIPS FOR NOTIONS

Here is just a sample of the many notions used in scrapbooking.

Buttons

Threads, string and twine

Ribbons and lace

Pins (hat pins, safety pins and dressmaking pins)

Hooks and eyes

Silk flowers, dried flowers and leaves

Beads, sequins and glitter

Fabric scraps

Charms

Costume jewellery

Twill (or cotton tape)

Hinges

Closures (buckles, D-rings, clasps)

COLLECTING NOTIONS

Sewing supply and haberdashery stores are a great source for notions, as are thrift or second-hand stores. Imaginative use of everyday items found in the home will extend your collection of notions even further.

The only limitation to using notions is that they need to be acid-free (as most fabrics are) or sprayed with an anti-acid agent.

Keen collectors of notions will check old clothes for useable parts like buttons or trimmings before throwing them out. Even the fabric itself can be used.

Notions are often handed down in the family and an old button box is a treasured find for the avid scrapbooker. Old-fashioned buttons and laces look especially lovely on heritage layouts and may themselves be a family heirloom.

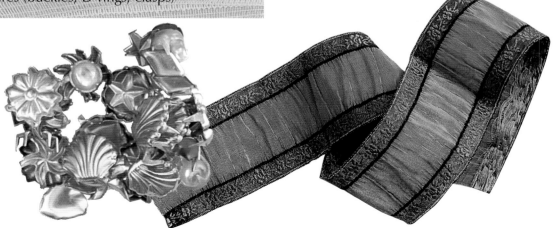

RIBBON, LACE AND THREAD

Ribbons and laces are easily acquired and have many uses. Use ribbon for a small bow to embellish a photo mat. Wrap ribbons and lace around the entire layout and tie in a bow to form a pretty border. Trim the edge of a heritage photo mat or journalling box with lace.

Small roses made from ribbon can be purchased ready-made in a rainbow of colours and they make attractive embellishments or borders.

Threads, string and twine are used to tie items to the page. They can also be wrapped around frames or small envelopes. Thread them through eyelets to form borders on layouts and photo mats or use them to hang tags.

A twisted ribbon made from your own combination of different kinds of fibres is a pretty and unique way to embellish a layout with some old-world style. See page 90 for step-by-step instructions.

BUTTONS AND FABRIC

Buttons are a favourite as they sit flat and can be sewn or glued to a layout.

Buttons can be used in a number of ways–as part of the title (such as a small button on top of the letter 'i'), sewn onto the corners of photos and journalling boxes, lined up to form a border or attached to a tag.

Choose fabrics for colour or texture according to the theme of the page. Use darker, rich-coloured fabrics for autumn and winter layouts, lighter pastels for spring and vibrant colours for summer.

Wrap fabric around a photo frame or use a heavily textured fabric (such as hessian) as a photo mat.

Tulle is a lightweight and effective fabric, especially evocative on wedding layouts. Lay a piece of tulle over one corner of the layout or use scraps of tulle to dress up die-cuts.

BEADS, SEQUINS AND GLITTER

Add some sparkle to your scrapbook layouts by gluing glitter or sequins to the edges of a photo mat or journalling box. Thread beads onto wire, pins or thin thread and stitch or glue to a layout element. Beads can also be dangled on a knotted thread from the bottom of a photo mat or title.

TWILL (COTTON TAPE)

Twill or cotton tape is used to tie items together in a bundle. Twill is very versatile as it can be dyed, stamped or imprinted, allowing you to change its colour to match the page.

Most computer printers will allow twill to be fed through easily, provided it is tightly secured to a piece of paper or cardstock. Follow the same instructions as for printing fonts on paper scraps (refer to the tips box in the section on Using Computers).

PINS AND HOOKS AND EYES

Use pins to attach tags to frames or mats. Pins are also good for attaching photos, paper or vellum to a page. Small beads can be threaded onto a safety pin or hat. Metal charms or alphabet letters look great hanging from pins.

Hooks and eyes can also be used to hang items from a frame or mat and as connectors for fibres.

CHARMS AND COSTUME JEWELLERY

Tiny charms, such as hearts, butterflies, flowers, keys or footballs, take on a special meaning when used on an appropriately themed page.

Charms can be tied with threads or fibres, attached with glue, threaded onto a pin or wire and attached with a jump ring or clip.

Broken jewellery or jewellery that is no longer in fashion can add a fun touch and special meaning to pages. Attach smaller jewellery items as you would attach charms.

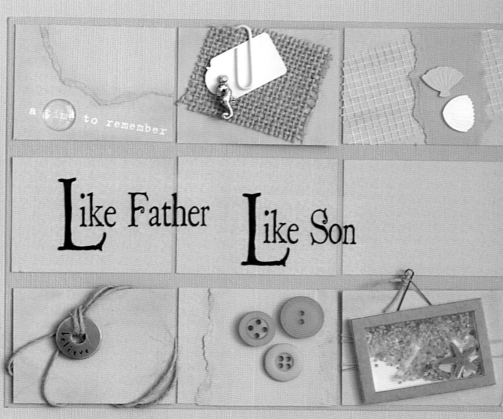

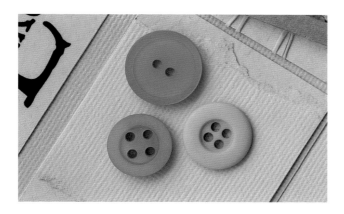

HINGES

Hinges come in many shapes and sizes and can be purchased from scrapbooking, hardware or craft stores. There are ornamental hinges (such as those used on jewellery box lids) or plainer, heavier hinges to choose from. They can be functional as well as decorative, and are used to create 'doors' on pages. Attach hinges with a strong silicone-based glue or crystal lacquer.

CLOSURES (BUCKLES, D-RINGS, AND CLASPS)

Thread ribbon or twill through a buckle or D-ring to form a closure for a mini-book on a page. Wrap fibres around one side of the page and use a clasp to connect them at the front. Use a small buckle to join two or more ribbons around a photo mat or journalling box.

1 Select four different types of fibres of varying textures, such as pearl string, ribbons and wool. After cutting the fibres to the same length, group and secure them together by wrapping tape around one end.

2 Begin twisting or plaiting the fibres together, starting from the taped end and working down the length. When the twisting is complete, tape the unsecured ends together to prevent the twist from unravelling.

3 Attach to the front of the layout using glue dots or small amounts of silicone glue so the twist is held in place. Wrap the ends over the top and bottom edges of the layout and adhere to the back with tape or glue.

Stitching

Sewing or stitching on scrapbook pages is a popular technique that adds an appealing home-made touch. Hand and machine stitching can be used as a decorative feature or in the construction of a layout, such as attaching memorabilia. Almost anything can be stitched including paper, fabric, buttons and even some thin metals.

HAND-STICHING TIPS

Vary the type of thread and length of stitches to create different effects.

Create unique titles by drawing letters or patterns in pencil and stitching over the top.

Hand stitch with wire instead of thread.

Pierce thin metal shapes or metal sheets with a pick and hand-stitch them to the page.

Hand-sew buttons or other lumpy items directly onto a page.

STITCHING ON LAYOUTS

Stitching can be used as an embellishment on a page or as a way of adding dimension any existing embellishments.

Stitching itself can form a frame around a photograph or a panel of journalling. If it is used around the edges of photo mats, stitching will provide extra definition. The outside edges of a page can also be highlighted this way–blanket stitching is particularly effective.

Stitching is also utilized in the construction of a layout. Elements such as memorabilia or embellishments can be attached to the page with discreet or decorative stitches. Two layers of paper can be stitched to each other to form a pocket.

A unique background can also be created by joining together two or more pieces of paper with stitching.

MACHINE-STITCHING

Cardstock can be sewn easily with any basic sewing machine. Just make sure to adjust the machine settings first.

Draw in stitching guidelines with a ruler and graphite pencil to help control the stitching. Carefully remove these markings when the stitching has been completed.

Experiment with different stitching techniques, such as straight, zigzag, blanket and running stitches, on your sewing machine.

A sewing machine will make stitching jobs easier, faster and provide an even appearance.

However, hand-stitching works just as well and

has some advantages that a sewing machine cannot offer. A delicate layout with many embellishments will often prove too cumbersome for a sewing machine.

discover

Discover the world around you

for this is nature's way

fine grains of sand and

grass embedded dunes

surrounds for you to play.

discover

HAND-STITCHING

Stitching by hand can result in either a neat or very 'handmade' finish, depending on the effect required.

If a more rustic look is wanted, consider stitching freehand to create uneven stitches in a slightly crooked line.

For a neater look with straight and even stitches the best method is to use a ruler and metal pick or large needle to pre-make the holes before stitching.

Specialized stitching placement tools, such as the 'Fiber Friend', are available. This will make the process easier as it has holes marked at regular intervals.

The wide variety of thread colours on the market makes it easier to colour-match any layout.

The best kinds of threads to use for scrap-booking projects are sewing and embroidery threads as they are archivally safe.

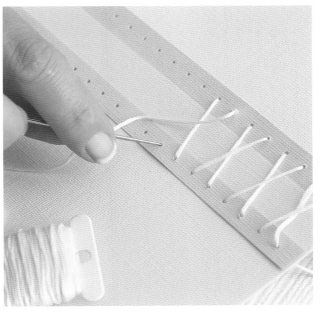

1 Using the ruler, mark the stitching points along a pencilled line, for example, about 1 cm or 1/4 inch apart. With a pick or needle, pierce the paper at each marked interval. An easier option is to use a stitching placement tool, as shown.

2 Use tape to anchor the thread's end to the back of the paper, near the starting point of the needle holes. Pass the needle and thread in and out of the needle holes, as you would through fabric, forming the cross pattern, as shown.

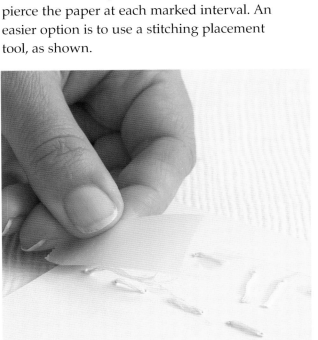

3 Once the end of the row of holes is reached, anchor the end of the thread to the back of the paper with sticky tape.

Using metals

Metal, in various forms, is frequently used in scrapbooking. Whether its purpose is functional or purely decorative, metal can add an element of texture or strength to a layout. Eyelets and brads have a particularly important function as they are used to attach elements, such as journal blocks or embellishments, to a layout.

METAL ACCENTS

A wide range of metal accents and embellishments is available for scrapbooking. Metal can be used in the background, as with metal sheets and metal mesh. It can be purely decorative, as with pages embellished by small metal charms.

Text is available in the form of metal alphabets, words, plaques, bookplates, tags and tiles.

Metals frames, photo corners and hinges can be used to hold photographs. The construction of a page also makes use of metal elements such as conchos, clips and other connectors, the most common being brads (split pins) and eyelets.

Eyelets come in many shapes, sizes and colours. They can be ornamental or used to anchor elements to a layout. Fibres, wire and twine can be threaded through the eyelet holes for added texture.

SETTING AN EYELET

To set an eyelet, you will need a hard, sturdy work surface, a cutting mat, a hole punch and hammer (the size depends on the eyelet size) and an eyelet setter.

Use a pencil to mark the spot on the cardstock for the eyelets. Pierce a hole on the mark using a hole punch that corresponds to the size of the eyelet.

Place the eyelet in the hole from the front side of the paper, then holding it in place, flip the paper over so the reverse side is up. The eyelet shaft should stick up through the hole.

ALTERING METAL ACCENTS

All metal items can be used straight from the packet, but most can be altered to capture the distinct design of a layout. Sanding and painting are common methods of altering metals.

Sand the metal with a shiny surface before painting to help the paint adhere. Colour can then be added with acrylic paints, permanent inks or rub-ons. Sand the metal accents for a distressed effect.

Give a soft, aged look to the metal by applying white or verdigris-coloured acrylic paint over its surface, using a dry paintbrush. Do not mix water with the paint as a thicker consistency works better. When the paint is dry to the touch, use a soft cloth or paper towel and lightly rub over the edges or rub in a few spots to reveal the metal surface. This looks especially effective on metal accents with raised patterns such as decorative frames and photo corners.

Place the tip of the eyelet setter into the top of the eyelet shaft and tap the end of the setter with the hammer a few times until the edges of the eyelet shaft roll back and sit flat against the paper.

Gently tap the back of the eyelet directly once or twice with a hammer to flatten any raised areas.

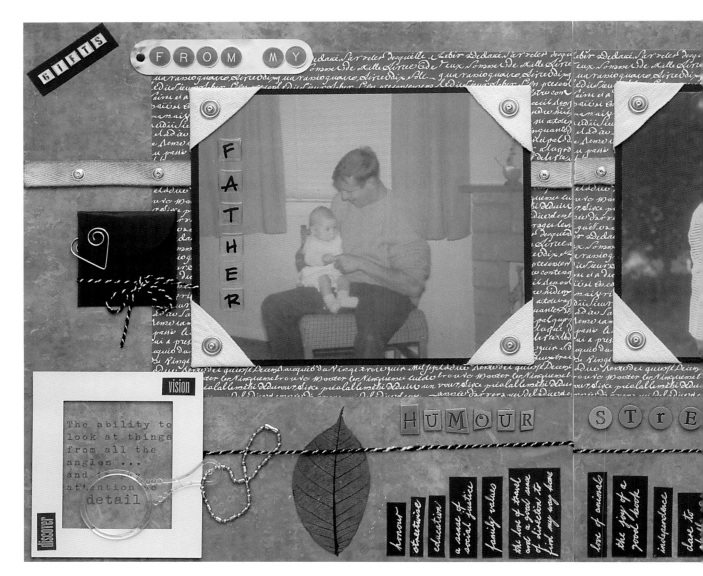

1 Sand the metal frame with a fine-grade sand-paper to prepare the surface for proper adhesion of the paint.

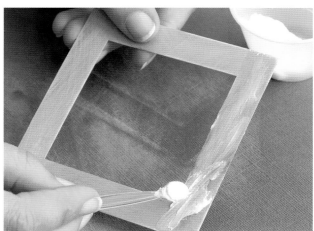

2 Prepare some thick white paint in a small cup or shallow dish without adding water. Paint the frame with a thin coat of paint using a brush or applicator.

3 Leave the painted frame to dry overnight. For added dimension, create a dark edge around the frame with an ink pad.

Image transfer and manipulation

Repeating an image on a page using a translucent or transparent medium emphasizes the mood or a detail of the original. You can create many different effects on a home computer, including printing on fabric, textured paper and matt or glossy surfaces. Here are a few ways of transfering photographs to other media.

COLOUR OR BLACK AND WHITE?

Printing digital images using a home computer is the easiest way to manipulate your photographs, including switching between black and white or colour with a single touch. However, it is possible to obtain similar effects using other means. Ask at your local photographic processing store about having colour prints reproduced in black and white, and enlarged or reduced in size at the same time. Alternatively, depending on the finish you require, a photocopier can produce a similar effect.

Using a large black-and-white image, as in the project opposite, focuses the attention on the facial expression of the subject. A smaller, translucent colour image adds detail that is not apparent in the big picture, without allowing the colours in the image to dictate the design of the layout.

TRANSFERRING IMAGES

There are several ways of transferring a photograph or image from opaque paper to a transparent or translucent material. You can print a photograph directly onto a transparency using a computer printer: use the printer software to select the transparency option. You need to ensure that the transparencies you use are designed for the type of printer and ink that you have.

Another simple method of transferring a photograph is to use an adhesive plastic, such as contact laminating sheets or packing tape. This method is suitable for laser prints and toner-based photocopies as well as magazine images, and is illustrated on the following pages.

Using artists' gel medium, it is possible to create a clear, softly textured finish on an inkjet photograph, then dissolve away the paper backing to create a translucent effect, as in the project opposite.

GEL MEDIUM

Gel medium is an artist medium used to increase the transparency and brilliance of acrylic paints without altering the consistency. It is an excellent binder and can be used with powdered pigments, as well as materials such as sand and sawdust to add texture. In some circumstances, it can also be used as an adhesive. You can find gel medium in art and craft stores.

Gel medium has a translucent white consistency when wet but dries clear with a smooth satin finish, making it ideal to use for transferring photographs, particularly inkjet prints that can't be transferred using other methods. Be creative and use a brush to add swirls or stripes in the gel to create a handpainted look on the finished image. Remember, the end result need not be a perfect copy of the original.

ADHESIVE PLASTIC

Various types of self-adhesive plastic film can be used to create transparent transfers from laser prints and copies as well as from magazine and newsprint pictures and text. Clear packing tape (the wide tape you use for sealing boxes and parcels) is one readily available form of adhesive plastic. The limited size of packing tape makes the transfers easy to work with and can provide interesting graphic opportunities; for example, to decorate tags. A long strip can be used as a border or, if you have a number of photographs you'd like to feature on one spread, you can assemble a comic-strip style collage on packing tape to provide a unifying treatment.

Contact laminating sheets, available from stationery stores, have a sticky surface under a removable backing that is designed to allow documents and photographs to be plastic-coated for protection without the need for a heat-laminating machine. Scrapbookers have discovered that the adhesive on contact laminating sheets fixes black laser printer and copying ink when the backing paper is gently dissolved, making wonderful transparent copies of photographs that can be used with striking effect on layouts.

The technique for dissolving the paper backing but leaving the image on the tramsparent plastic is similar for both of these materials. Other adhesive plastic materials may work in the same way.

You can experiment with different images and with the amount of the backing paper you remove to create other transparent and translucent effects.

1 Choose the image you wish to transfer using gel medium. The image used in this project is a colour photograph, inkjet printed on watercolour paper. Gel medium also works with magazine images, laser prints, postcards and cards. Use the same technique as shown here.

2 Place the photograph face up. Apply one coat of gel medium evenly over the image. For a smooth finish, use an expired credit card to sweep a thin layer of medium across the photograph. You can use a foam brush or a bristle brush to add texture. When the first layer is dry, repeat the gel application five times. Allow the final coat to dry overnight.

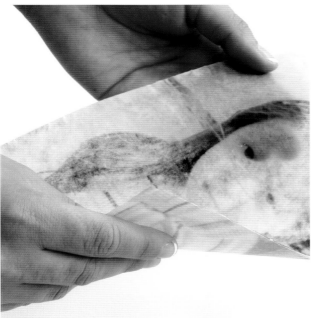

3 Soak the photograph in warm water. Rub away the paper on the back of the image with your fingers–the wet paper should form small crumbs and start to come away. Rub carefully so that you don't damage the image on the gel. you should now have a translucent image. Allow the image to dry; place a heavy object on top if the image starts to curl.

TRANSPARENCY TIPS

Transferring images onto transparent or translucent materials gives more options for display as the background behind the transparency becomes part of the image. Whether the background is coloured or textured cardstock, printed paper or fabric, the image takes on a three-dimensional appearance with literally more layers of meaning.

Printing images directly onto transparencies is one way to achieve this look, but you can simply use self-adhesive plastic film, a method that achieves the same effect with-out requiring a computer and printer.

The tag on the left is made with an image transferred onto a piece of clear packing tape. The word 'hiver' on the tag (meaning 'winter' in French) was created with black alphabet stickers and the image–taken from a magazine photograph–was transferred onto the tape using the method shown below, then positioned on the tag. The packing tape adhesive remains strong enough to hold the image in place.

1 You can use small images or photographs, parts of photographs, sections of pattern or even columns of text. Simply apply the packing tape smoothly over the area of printed or photo-copied material that you want to use. Trim away excess paper and tape.

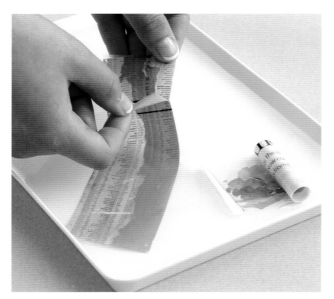

2 Soak the tape strips in a shallow container of tepid water for a few minutes. The tape will curl, so turn the pieces over and flatten them out several times during the soaking process. When the paper is quite wet, you can peel away most of the paper, leaving a translucent layer of pulp and the printed image.

3 Continue to rub away the paper pulp on the back of the tape with your fingers–doing this while the tape is still soaking in the water allows the paper crumbs to float away. When all the paper has been removed, pat the tape with paper towels or a soft cloth and allow it to dry completely before using it on a layout.

happiness

full of joy

have fun

come out and play

Oscar and Byron love it when their cousins, Fletcher and Spencer, come down from Sydney for the weekend. The boys spend hours in the pool, chase each other with water pistols, build cubby houses, explore the bush with Zoe, their dog, ride their bikes, and have endless turf-of-oh battles on their gameboys.
April 2003 - Woodlands Park

1 To transfer an image onto an adhesive laminating sheet, photocopy the photograph in black and white or print it on ordinary paper using a laser printer. Peel the backing paper off the laminate sheet and carefully place the photocopied image face down on the adhesive. Use a wooden craft stick to rub the back of the paper and ensure good adhesion all over.

2 Place the image in a shallow tray of water and allow it to soak for a few minutes. Remove it from the water and pat dry. With the plastic sheet face down, use your finger to rub the paper in small circular motions until it begins to form crumbs and come away from the plastic. Work gently in small sections and spritz with water if it becomes too dry to work. Rinse and gently pat dry.

3 Cut white cardstock squares to highlight the children's faces in the photograph and stick them to the back of the transparent image. The remaining contact adhesive should be enough to hold them in place. A light mist of spray adhesive can be used, if required. Complete the page with a line of black-and-white woven ribbon and journalling of your choice.

Fabric and textiles

Textiles such as woven fabric, ribbon, lace and fibres enhance scrapbook layouts by adding texture, softness, colour and dimension to the page. There's no limit to the range of patterns and colours that you can use, and you can even incorporate pieces of favourite clothing or samples of furnishing and dressmaking fabrics from special places and occasions.

STIMULATING THE SENSES

Treat woven fabric as you would paper or card-stock. If you want the fabric to sit flat, it is a good idea to use a fusible web backing such as an iron-on interfacing or stiffener to help the fabric sit firm

and flat on the page. Choose a fairly stiff web and follow the manufacturer's instructions for fusing before you cut the fabric to size.

Fabrics with interesting textures, such as even-weave linen, corduroy and hessian bring dimension to a flat layout. Silks and synthetic fabrics can be gathered, draped and twisted without adding too much bulk to the layout.

Ribbons and fibres of all shapes and sizes are suitable to be glued flat to the page or tied in bows or knots and left to hang. Ribbons can be used as part of the background design, or tied in strategic places to highlight features of the page.

SEWING CARDSTOCK

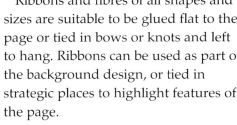

Most scrapbookers find that stranded embroidery cotton or rayon thread is suitable for handstitching on layouts. Use six strands together so that the large stitches are quite clearly visible. Wool is also suitable, although you may need to use a larger awl and needle to ensure that the paper will take the thicker ply.

When machine stitching, you can use an ordinary sewing machine with little or no adjustment. If the machine is also used for dressmaking or quilt piecing, it is a good idea to keep a separate needle for sewing paper and card. Practise on scraps of card and paper to select a loose tension that keeps the stitching flat, and make the stitches at least 3-4 mm (1/8 in) long so that the cardstock doesn't tear along the stitching line.

Many scrapbookers find that it is useful to purchase a small sewing machine that they keep solely for their paper crafts.

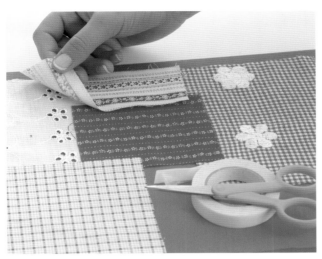

1 Select six different patterned pieces of colour-coordinated fabrics. Cut five pieces in different sizes and shapes and arrange them on a cardstock background, leaving a narrow border of cardstock around the resulting square of fabrics.

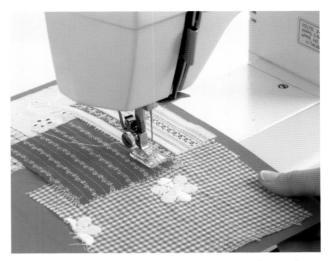

2 Use a sewing machine to stitch the edges of the fabric inside the square. A large zigzag stitch in contrasting or matching sewing thread looks great. Use the remaining fabric as a mat for the feature photograph. Position the photograph and mat on top of the stitched fabrics and stitch down the edges of the mat fabric with zigzag stitch.

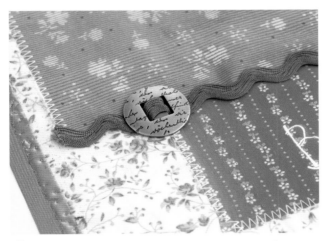

3 Add decorative metal photo corners and a border of rickrack or ribbon threaded through a metal buckle along the bottom edge of the fabric mat. Place heat-resistant, double-sided adhesive tape around the edges of the fabric collage to secure them to the cardstock, then sprinkle ultra-thick embossing enamel over the tape and heat-set.

FABRIC TO PAPER

Some papers are printed with photographs of fabric designs and other textures. These can be easier to work with than the original fabrics and finishes such as painted crackle finishes, as they don't require flattening, stiffening, specific cutting tools or other special treatments.

To add dimension and texture to pages that use printed papers rather than three-dimensional fabrics and painted textures, ribbons are a neat and pretty textile embellishment. Many scrapbook supply stores sell ribbons in colour-coordinated packs just as they do papers, cardstock and other embellishments, and these can be a great source of inspiration. Stitching paper down enhances the illusion of the three-dimensional texture that is printed on it, and the addition of pretty bows does the same.

Any type of ribbon is suitable for use on a scrapbook page: woven organza and satin; jacquard designs; stitched or printed patterns; gingham; paper and mulberry paper strips; dyed silk; wire-edged; and gift-wrap ribbons.

PAPER TIP

The papers used on this page are all selected from a coordinated range of vintage-look printed patterns that mimic fabric designs and paint textures. Complementary colours (opposite each other on the colour wheel) balance each other and accentuate the neutral tones of the black-and-white photograph. A linen-textured cardstock provides a backdrop for the pretty roses and ribbons.

1 Use white gesso to paint the outside edges of the cardstock: use a dry brush and bold sweeping strokes to apply the paint. Ink the edges of the cardstock to accentuate the gesso. Layer the papers and cut some pieces or tear some and roll the edges to give a variety of textures. Stitch the paper down using a machine zigzag stitch in selected places.

2 Use walnut ink and an old toothbrush to age the small tags. Lay the tags on a flat, protected surface and dip the toothbrush in the ink. Flick the bristles with your thumb to splatter ink over the tags. If the droplets are too large, blot with absorbent paper. Add journalling with an acid-free pen and tie pretty ribbons through the tags.

3 Sand the edges of the photograph using medium abrasive paper. Paint a cardstock mat in the same way as you painted the edges of the background cardstock and add machine stitching as a decorative border. Add embellishments, including the large chiffon bow and decorative photo corner.

FUSIBLE WEB

Fabric stiffener that is fused to the reverse of the fabric with an iron is useful for any fabrics that need to sit flat on a scrapbook layout. There are many different types of fusible web (iron-on stiffener) that you can use for this purpose, and most are inexpensive.

The best type is a fairly stiff interfacing that is fusible on one side only. You don't need double-sided fusible web as you will use acid-free adhesive, glue, photo tabs or double-sided adhesive tape to secure the fabric to the scrapbook page, as well as other methods of fastening.

If you choose an interfacing with a similar weight to paper you can use the stiffened fabric as you would treat paper, cutting it with scissors or a paper trimmer, inserting eyelets or brads, stapling, stitching and gluing.

FRAYED EDGES

Woven fabric tends to fray when cut. You can use frayed fabric as a feature of the page–it looks particularly good if you use coarse fabrics like hessian or linen, but can be fun with fine silks and synthetic fabrics too.

If you want a neat finished edge, there are several ways to prevent fraying. Fusible web has the advantage of preventing frayed edges if you use this type of stiffener. You can apply liquid fray stopper that you paint on with a small brush; this is useful for woven ribbons too. In an emergency, clear nail polish can be used.

Stitching down the edges of the fabric with a zigzag stitch is another way to prevent fraying. Old-fashioned hemming by hand or with a sewing machine can be done before gluing fabric to the page if you don't want to stitch through the background cardstock.

ACID-FREE FABRIC

Fabric and fibres are generally acid-free or so low in acid-causing lignin that the amount is negligible–even plant-based fibres such as hemp, linen and cotton are basically acid- and lignin-free.

Natural fibres need to be protected from the effects of the environment in the same way as paper, so an archival-quality adhesive, embellishment and storage system is still essential if you want to preserve your scrapbook album for a long period of time.

If fabric has been used or worn prior to being placed in the scrapbook it is a good idea to wash it in mild detergent before using it on a layout.

Acid-free fabric glue is available from specialty scrapbook suppliers and many craft stores.

FUN WITH FIBRES

Narrow ribbons, fancy knitting yarns and textured embroidery threads can be threaded through eyelets and tags, wrapped around layouts and embellishments, stitched down in straight and curved lines and glued onto pages to highlight textures and shapes in a photograph. You can have lots of fun with textured yarns such as chenille, shaggy yarns and synthetic or real mohair threads.

Serendipity squares

Serendipity squares complement the theme of a page, although they are not an integral part of the journalling, title, images or memorabilia. They have a serendipitous (desirable but unplanned) association with the main elements of the page, by their colour, texture, subject or even the motifs they include. Beads, bows and charms add depth and interest.

1 This scrapbook page has an obvious beach theme that is complemented by the embellishments and serendipity box. Create a water-like border for the title block using metallic blue ultra-thick embossing enamel. Apply double-sided heat-resistant tape around all four edges of the panel, ensuring the ends of the tape meet closely.

2 Remove the backing from the tape to reveal the sticky surface. Pour metallic blue ultra-thick embossing enamel powder onto the tape. Heat the crystals with a heat gun until they have melted and allow the enamel to dry. You only need one layer of embossing powder to create the liquid look of the finished border.

SERENDIPITY SHAPES

The simplest and most traditional serendipity square is a collage of coloured paper scraps; however, you can take these embellishments to a new creative dimension by using a variety of craft techniques. Although these decorative elements are often called serendipity squares they don't have to be square, or even rectangular—you can make them circular, triangular, polygonal, irregular or any shape you like.

Select a piece of textured card, fabric, plastic, glass or metal to be the background. Apply a finish if you like: for example, sanding, acrylic paint and crackle medium, embossed metal or card or adding ultra-thick embossing enamel.

Now search for embellishments that complement the story that your page is telling. Scout through bric-a-brac at garage sales and second-hand stores for inspiration. You need to find items that inject a sense of the moment into the layout.

serendipity (ser'ən dip'ə te), *n.* a seeming gift for finding something good accidentally (*Webster's New World College Dictionary*, Third Edition, Macmillan, 1988)

3 Add an embossed strip to the sides of the metal letter tiles for the title in the same manner: apply a strip of double-sided heat-resistant tape, remove the backing, then sprinkle liberally with ultra-thick embossing enamel. Apply heat to melt the crystals and allow to cool.

4 Emboss a piece of copper shim using this simple ageing method: lay the metal on a rough concrete or stone surface and tap it with a hammer until you achieve the desired effect.

5 Since this layout has a beach theme, the contents of the memory bottle appear to have come from the sea shore. You could collect and wash some sand from the beach, or purchase clean sand from a craft store. Add a selection of mini sequins and faux pearls to the mixture. Scoop or siphon the mix into the bottle until it is almost full. Insert the stopper with a drop or two of silicone to seal it.

6 Decorate the neck of the bottle with wire threaded with faux pearls and beads. To secure the bottle to the page, set two eyelets a short distance apart through the metal shim and into the cardstock. Thread a piece of wire through the holes, then around the neck of the bottle, and secure with adhesive tape on the reverse of the layout.

The world is your oyster

celebrate

e
i
g
h
t

2003

2 0 0 3

Georgie (with Talena) Broadbeach Qld.

August 8 th Birthday

Collage Collections

The conglomeration of intriguing ephemera that characterizes the collage style of scrapbooking looks almost as though it has been gathered up and scattered at random on the page. Far from being haphazard, the layouts on the following pages are painstakingly constructed using carefully selected embellishments.

PRESENTING PHOTOGRAPHS

Photographs on collage-style layouts are rarely centred neatly on mats, so finding creative ways to attach and display photographs to the page is part of the fun of this style of scrapbooking.

Sometimes the subject of the photographs will suggest a unique method of fastening: photographs of a child on a swing are suspended from a wire line by miniature hanging clips, an echo of the suspension of a swing. In other cases, the style of the collage will supply the answer: slip a photograph behind the ribbons of a mock French noticeboard. Another solution is to simply adhere the photograph to the page unmatted–there is so much happening on the page as it is that the photograph does not need any other visual anchor.

STACKING IT UP

Collage layouts are created by assembling an inspired collection of cardstock, paper, ephemera and embellishments, then stacking the items from largest to smallest, at the same time creating balance with colour, shape and effect.

It's a process of addition and subtraction, so it's wise to lay it all out before applying any permanent adhesive. Some sections of the collage may be miniature collages in themselves, requiring assembly before they are placed on the page.

There are almost no rules about what can be used on a collage layout: the three-dimensional nature of the style means that found objects and lumpy decorations are just as appropriate as flat embellishments. Alter objects such as buttons, dominoes and game pieces, tiles and tags to blend with the collage, using paint, stamps, stickers, embossing enamel and clear dimensional adhesive.

UP close, photo by a very patient Daddy 2004

MASS OR MESS?

If you have never made a collage you might wonder how to stop a mass of embellishments from looking like a mess. One trick is to group most of the items together in one part of the page, allowing the photograph or photographs to occupy uncrowded space.

Another tip is to keep the collage elements to one main colour, plus neutrals such as black or beige. Keep scraps of fabric, ribbon and fibres in zip-lock bags according to colour and, if necessary, use ink or acrylic paints to change the colour of some embellishments to suit a particular collage.

Keep good design theory in mind and layer the collage so that your eye follows a path around the page.

1 A French noticeboard looks elegant and it's easy to create the effect on a scrapbook layout. You can arrange photographs and other embellishments around the lattice of ribbons, tucking them underneath or pinning them in place. Start with a sheet of scrap card the same size as your background paper or card and mark out a diagonal grid of squares about 7 cm (2¾ in) wide.

2 Place the grid on top of the patterned paper or card for the background and use paperclips to hold the two layers together. Place a foam rubber mat underneath and use an awl, a large needle or a paper piercer to make small holes where the lines intersect, through both layers of card or paper.

3 Remove the card with the grid and weave the ribbons across the page, using the pierced holes as guides to where they should cross under and over. Secure the ribbon ends at the edges of the page with double-sided adhesive tape (you can cover this with a cardstock frame). Anchor the lattice by setting decorative snaps or brads into the pierced holes, pushing them through the ribbon.

FOUND OBJECTS

You can use wire rig links from a fishing tackle store to provide a clothesline effect, from which you can hang photographs and embellishments using miniature metal clips. Attach the rig links to the layout using metal brads and nailheads through the loops at the end of the wire rig. As well as the miniature metal clips, use wire loops and small safety pins to attach beads, charms and tags to the wire.

1 You can use game pieces such as letter or number tiles and dominoes to make a three-dimensional title. On the back of the game piece, apply a coat of clear-drying adhesive with a paintbrush. Smooth a piece of printed tissue paper over the adhesive and allow to dry.

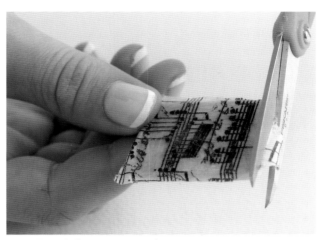

2 Carefully cut away the excess tissue paper with sharp, pointed scissors, then lightly sand the edges to remove any excess paper. Apply another coat of clear-drying adhesive and allow to dry.

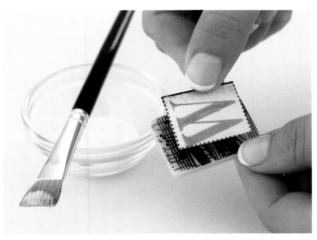

3 Use an alphabet sticker or letter cut-out for each game piece to spell out the words of the title. Ink around the edges of the letter before applying it to the game piece. Glue the letter to the game piece and apply a final coat of clear-drying adhesive over the top. Attach the game piece to the layout with double-sided adhesive tape or acid-free liquid adhesive.

Metals and minerals

Incorporating metals and minerals such as mica, shim, gold leaf, metal tiles and even glass into your scrapbook pages allows you to create interesting effects on your layouts. Some of these materials require special tools and careful attention, while others are easy to work with using tools you already own.

METAL

Using metal on a scrapbook layout is hardly unusual, as this material features in many embellishments from eyelets and brads to staples, wire and metallic paper. Using thin metal sheets, such as copper, brass or aluminium shim, is similar to using paper or cardstock. These materials can be worked with paper scissors and trimmers; they can be punched to take eyelets or have shapes punched out of them; they can be embossed with a stylus, curled around a wooden skewer or even stitched onto the page. Shim of various thicknesses (gauge) is available in coloured finishes as well as traditional copper, brass, steel and aluminium.

Gold and silver leaf can add opulence to special layouts and, while the materials can be expensive, they can be used judiciously to create wonderful effects. Apply metal leaf directly onto cardstock, use it over wet ink to highlight stamped designs, or add precious metal touches to inexpensive embellishments.

1 Choose a piece of mica to make your frame. An irregular shape creates a pleasing effect. Tear the outer edge of the mica to create the desired shape, if necessary. You will find that the sheets of mica can be easily separated by slipping a fingernail between the layers and gently peeling them apart.

2 Use acid-free ink or pens to add extra colour to the mica. You can sandwich ink between layers and move the layers around to blur the still-wet ink. Place a photograph under the mica, then use a pen to mark a point on the photograph just inside each corner. These points will be your cutting guides.

MICA

Mica is a naturally occurring silicate material. It sometimes crystallizes into sheets, which can be separated into layers of different thicknesses. Mica can come in many different colours such as grey, yellow, green, red, brown or transparent.

It is photo-friendly, as it does not contain acid or lignin that will cause paper and photographs to fade and become brittle. The natural variations in colour and density add to the effect that is created on the page.

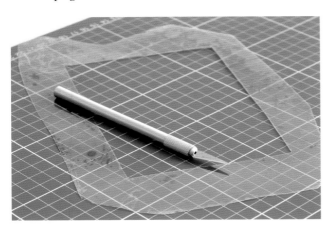

3 Use a craft knife and ruler to cut out the centre of the frame. If you feel confident, cutting freehand gives a looser, more natural effect as the lines are not perfectly straight. Glue the photograph to the background and fasten the mica frame over the top.

WORKING WITH MICA

You can vary the colour intensity of mica by separating the layers. Use your fingernail to push gently on the edge of the top layer until it begins to separate. Peel the layers apart until the mica is the desired thickness. The thinner the mica sheet, the more flexible it is and the more translucent. Mica can be cut with a paper trimmer, scissors or a knife; it can also be torn and punched with craft punches.

Attach mica as you would attach a transparency or vellum, using invisible adhesive or hiding the adhesive under other embellishments. You can be creative in the way you attach it. Mica easily accepts eyelets, brads, staples, conchos, safety pins and other fastening embellishments.

Stamp, gild and emboss mica as you would other smooth materials such as a transparency. Be sure to allow sufficient drying time for the ink. While mica will not burn or melt, it may be discoloured by too much heat.

MICA TIPS

Use mica on your scrapbook pages to create unusual effects:

| mat a photograph or create a translucent overlay to accentuate parts of the image

| stamp, emboss or gild the mica

| frame a photograph

| highlight words or an image with pieces of mica

| create faux tiles

| use a thin transparent layer in a frame or slide mount as a lightweight alternative to glass and perspex

| place ink between two layers of mica to change texture and colour

| sandwich flat items between two layers to hold them in place and preserve them.

PAINTED METAL

Metal embellishments can be painted and decorated to suit a scrapbook page. It is important when decorating metal to remember that it has a smooth surface that will not absorb water. This means that acrylic paint won't adhere to the surface easily.

Small metal pieces such as brads and metal frames that won't be handled often can be painted with acrylic paint; however, if you want an opaque finish it's a good idea to paint the metal with a coat of gesso first. A light sanding with fine abrasive paper will also provide a key in the metal surface to help the paint adhere.

Metal can also be stamped or coloured with ink, although you may need to experiment with different types of ink for the best results. Some inks will not adhere to metal at all, while others may need to be set with a heat tool. All-purpose inks such as StazOn™ will usually adhere to metal.

METAL LEAF

Applying delicate sheets of precious metal to a surface is an operation that requires some skill and practice. For basic gilding (application of metal leaf) you will need a base coat, metal-leaf adhesive, metal leaf, a pair of soft cotton gloves, a soft bristle brush and a sealer coat.

To prepare the surface for metal leaf, a base coat of red paint is traditionally applied. Unless you want to leave some of the surface exposed, the colour of the base coat is not important, nor is its presence essential.

Metal leaf adhesive is normally a milky liquid that dries clear and tacky after 10 minutes. Follow the manufacturer's instructions when working with this adhesive.

Wear cotton gloves when working with metal leaf to prevent it from being contaminated with the oils from your skin. Use your fingers and a soft bristle brush to apply small pieces of metal leaf, smoothing it with the brush as you go.

When the surface is completely covered, buff the metal with a soft cloth to remove any loose pieces and add shine. Coat the leaf with sealer to protect the surface and to prevent tarnishing.

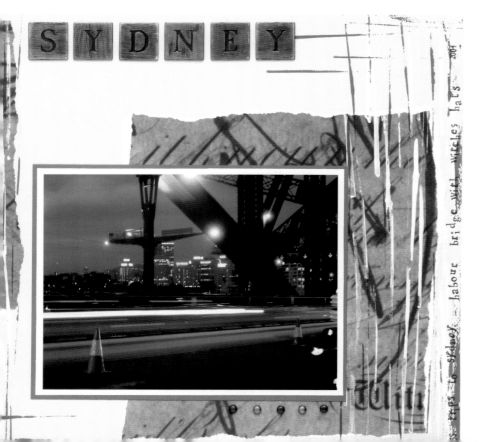

1 Using suitable adhesive for the metal leaf, swipe some strokes over the background cardstock. Allow the adhesive to dry until it is just tacky to touch, then apply the silver leaf over the adhesive. Brush away any extra metal leaf with a soft paintbrush.

2 Use a computer word-processing program to type a selection of words using differing text sizes and fonts. Make the background black and change the text to white. Reverse the image and print onto a transparency sheet. When the ink on the transparency is dry, cut out a 15 cm (6 in) diameter circle, selecting a section where the silver leaf highlights particular words.

3 Glue the transparency circle over the silver leaf and smooth with a soft cloth to ensure it lies flat. Cut a 6 cm (2¼ in) diameter circle from the transparency, centred on a key word. Use the same silver-leaf application method as before to make a single strip that highlights the main word in the smaller circle.

Project makers

Published in 2005 by Bay Books, an imprint of Murdoch Books Pty Limited.

Editor: Anouska Jones
Designer: Nanette Backhouse, saso content & design
Additional layout: Jenny Mansfield
Photographer: Ian Hofstetter
Stylist: Anne-Maree Unwin
Authors: Frank Saraco; Louise Riddell
Additional Text: Joanne Green; Leanne Hand
Scrapbooking Consultants: Joanne Green; Leanne Hand; Louise Riddell; Frank Saraco
Template Design and Illustration: Spatchurst
Additional Illustration: Tricia Oktober; Tracy Loughlin; Isn't She Clever Design and Illustration
Production: Megan Alsop

ISBN 0 681 06687 3.

Printed by Sing Cheong Printing Company Ltd. PRINTED IN CHINA.
First printed in 2005. Second Edition 2005.
© Text, photography, design and illustrations Murdoch Books Pty Limited 2005.

Acknowledgements
The publisher would like to thank the following for supplying products for photography:
Scrapbook Cottage, 2/8 Victoria Avenue, Castle Hill NSW 2154, www.scrapbookcottage.com.au

Circle template

Oval template

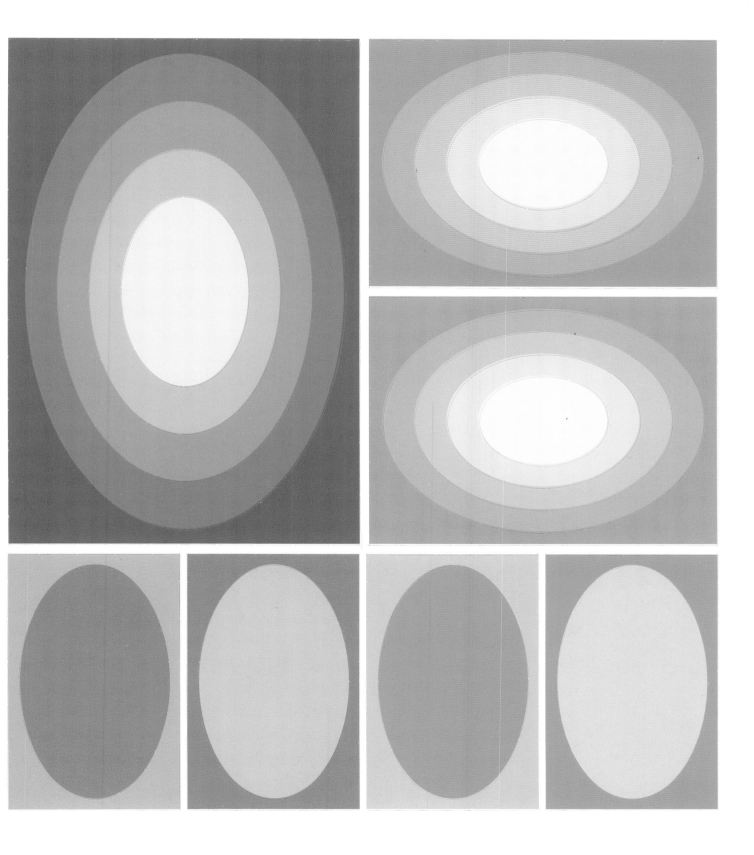

Uppercase stencil

ABCDEF
GHIJKL
MNOPQ
RSTUV
WXYZ?!

Lowercase stencil

abcdefg
hijklmn
opqrstu
vwxyz?!

Uppercase letters

A A A A B B B C C
C D D D E E E F
F F G G G H H H I
I I I J J J K K K
L L L M M M N N N
O O O O P P P Q Q
Q R R R S S S T T
T U U U V V V W W
W X X X Y Y Y Z Z

. . .. ' ' ^ Ç ? !

a	a	a	b	b	b	c	c
d	d	d	e	e	e	e	f
f	g	g	g	h	h	h	i
i	i	j	j	j	k	k	k
l	l	m	m	m	n	n	n
o	o	o	p	p	p	q	q
r	r	r	s	s	s	t	t
u	u	u	v	v	v	w	w
x	x	x	y	y	y	z	z
.	¨	´	,	^	ç	?	!

Traceable alphabet

a b c d e f g h i j k l m n

o p q r s t u v w x y z

1 2 3 4 5 6 7 8 9 0

` ´ ¨ ^ ~ ç ø & ? ! " "

A B C D E F G

H I J K L L M N

O P Q R S T U

V W X Y Z

Tags and reinforces

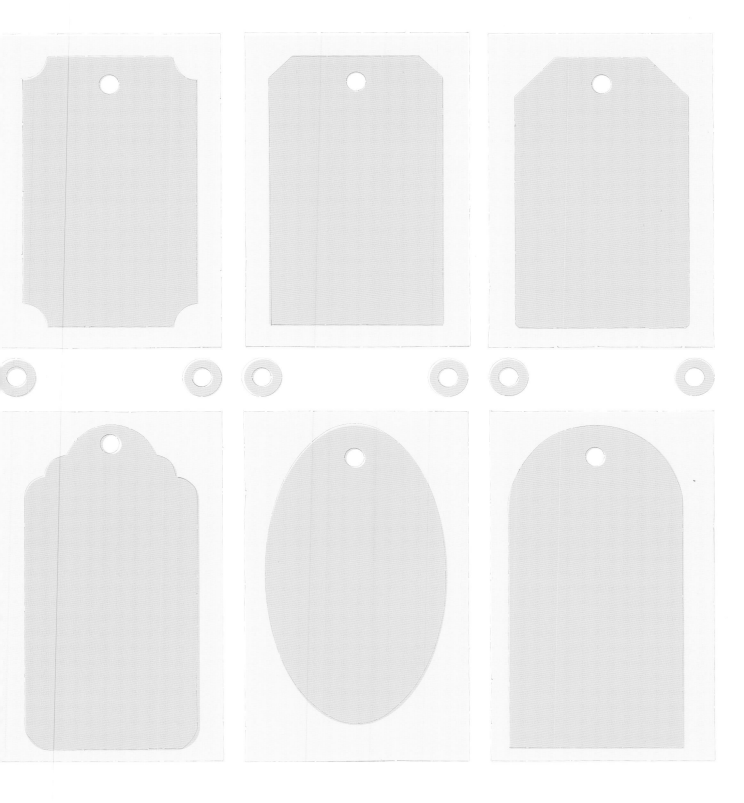

Frames

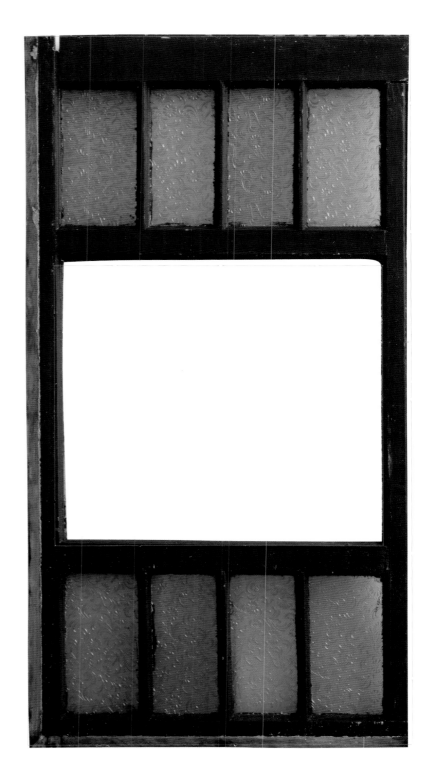

Frames

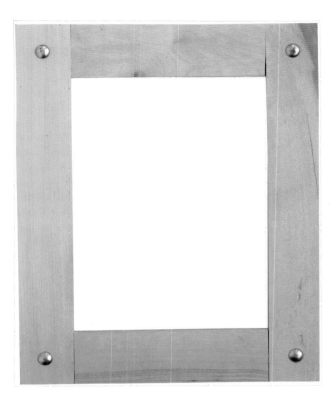

Textures

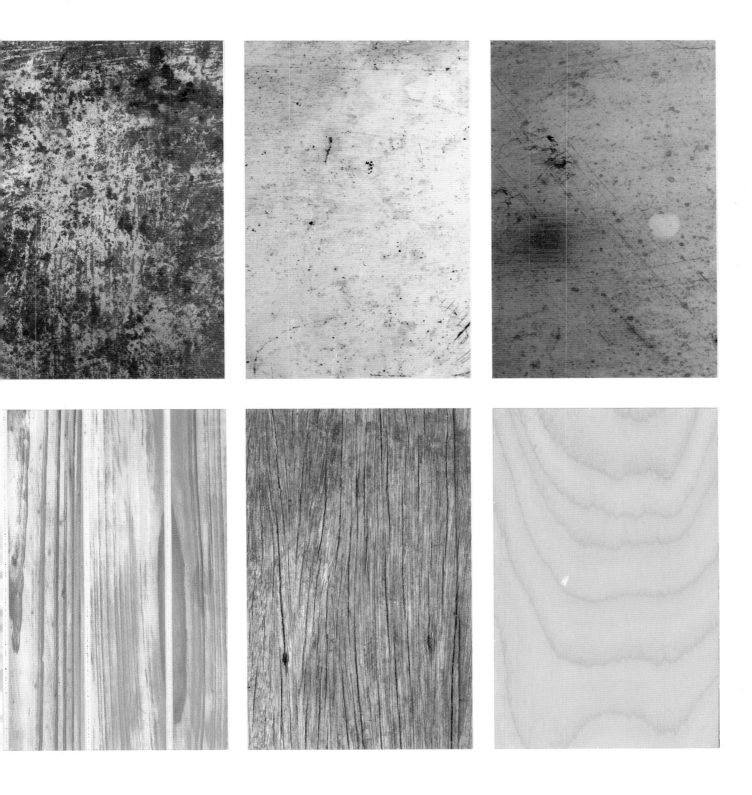

Metals

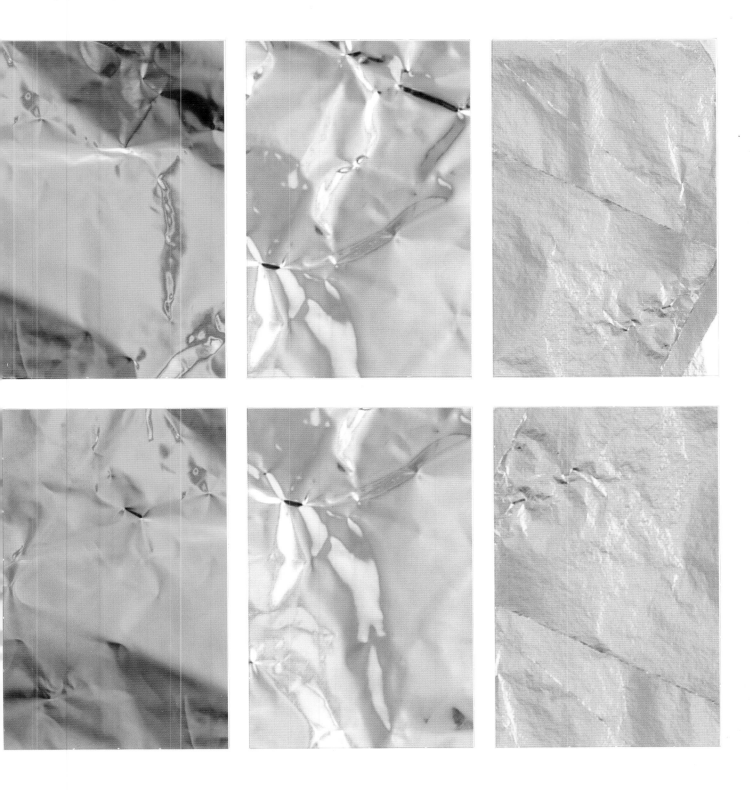